JESUS

NAME ABOVE ALL NAMES

Text copyright © Anne Le Tissier 2012
The author asserts the moral right
to be identified as the author of this work

Published by
The Bible Reading Fellowship
15 The Chambers, Vineyard
Abingdon OX14 3FE
United Kingdom
Tel: +44 (0)1865 319700
Email: enquiries@brf.org.uk
Website: www.brf.org.uk
BRF is a Registered Charity

ISBN 978 0 85746 085 1

First published 2011
10 9 8 7 6 5 4 3 2 1 0
All rights reserved

Acknowledgments
Bible studies first published in *Woman Alive*, the magazine for today's Christian woman:
www.womanalive.co.uk

Unless otherwise stated, scripture quotations are taken from the Holy Bible, New International
Version, copyright © 1973, 1978, 1984, 1995 by International Bible Society, are used by
permission of Hodder & Stoughton Publishers, a member of the Hachette Livre Group UK.
All rights reserved. 'NIV' is a registered trademark of International Bible Society. UK trademark
number 1448790.

Scripture quotations marked ESV are from the Holy Bible, English Standard Version, published
by HarperCollins Publishers © 2001 Crossway Bibles, a division of Good News Publishers.
Used by permission. All rights reserved.

Scripture taken from the Holy Bible, Today's New International Version®. Copyright © 2001,
2005 by Biblica®. Used by permission of Biblica®. All rights reserved worldwide.

Scripture quotations from THE MESSAGE. Copyright © by Eugene H. Peterson 1993, 1994,
1995. Used by permission of NavPress Publishing.

Scripture taken from the Holman Christian Standard Bible ® Copyright © 2003, 2002, 2000,
1999 by Holman Bible Publishers. All rights reserved.

The paper used in the production of this publication was supplied by mills that source their
raw materials from sustainably managed forests. Soy-based inks were used in its printing and
the laminate film is biodegradable.

A catalogue record for this book is available from the British Library

Printed in Singapore by Craft Print International Ltd

JESUS

NAME ABOVE ALL NAMES

32 BIBLE STUDIES ON THE
PERSON AND WORK OF JESUS

ANNE LE TISSIER

CONTENTS

FOREWORD

We were coming to the end of a very successful series about the women of the Bible and the question loomed: what next? Our Bible studies had become an important part of *Woman Alive* magazine and highly valued by readers, so the pressure was on.

As I considered and prayed about it, I kept coming back to the person of Jesus. Having focused on many different biblical characters, perhaps it was time to focus on him.

I thought about the images he used to describe himself—the good shepherd, the bread of life, the vine—and then images used by others: Isaiah's foretelling of the King of kings and the apostle John's picture of an advocate for us in heaven. I mused not only on what these tell us about Jesus, but also the kind of response they may require of us.

Anne, who had written a number of articles for our previous series, shared my enthusiasm. She developed the idea, providing not only helpful information but also searching questions that are rooted in real life.

Studying the names and descriptions of Jesus is not a new idea, but it's certainly a rich source of study. It is our prayer that through these studies, readers from all walks of life might be drawn into a deeper relationship with him and a greater understanding of the person and character of our Lord and Saviour.

Jackie Harris
Editor, *Woman Alive*

JESUS:

OUR ADVOCATE WITH THE FATHER

I have a confession to make! About 17 years ago, while living in a town flat in Guernsey, I returned home late one cold winter's night, parked the car in the only remaining space and dashed indoors to my cosy bed. While getting ready the next morning, however, a commotion in the road outside drew my attention to a long tailback of traffic, unusual even at rush hour in that part of town.

It was only as I left the building and began walking past those frustrated, angry drivers that I realised what was causing the hold-up. A large pickup truck was blocking the one-way system, with a couple of burly men rigging up tow-ropes to my car.

Yes—it was one of those unforgettable, stomach-churning moments, when I suddenly realised my mistake. In my hurry to get indoors the night before, I'd failed to notice I was parked across a delivery entrance, clearly marked with a sign: 'PARKING PROHIBITED between the hours of 7am and 6pm'. I was caught 'red cheeked'! The constable took my details, my car was unhooked, the pickup gave way to the snarled-up cars, and I was eventually allowed to drive away, then await my summons to court.

As it happens, however, I never actually went. A close friend, who happened to be an advocate, kindly offered to take my place, admit the offence and pay the fine on my behalf.

Whether or not you've ever had need of an advocate to complete a house sale, register a bond, represent or defend you, the apostle John reminds us of our advocate in heaven. 'I write this to you,' John says, 'so that you will not sin. But if anybody does sin, we have an advocate with the Father— Jesus Christ, the Righteous One' (1 John 2:1, TNIV). The older NIV translates the word 'advocate' as 'one who speaks to the Father in our defence'.

Indeed, it is his very righteousness (not a law degree), that qualifies him for the role, for 'he is the atoning sacrifice for our sins' (v. 2). Nor does he only ever plead our innocence; rather, he acknowledges to our Father those things we admit we've done wrong, then presents himself—his righteous sacrifice—on our behalf.

WHEN WE SIN UNINTENTIONALLY

I unwittingly broke the law. I parked my car without checking that it could remain there past 7am. The penalty had to be paid. Without such a friend, I would have had to go to court, face the judge and pay the penalty myself. In that instance, however, I had a friend who was willing to acknowledge the offence on my behalf and presented his own cheque to pay my fine.

As believers in Christ for salvation from spiritual death,

we have already been justified before God and adopted as his children. Furthermore, Jesus, who has become our friend (Luke 5:20; John 15:13–15), commands that we stop sinning (Matthew 5:48; John 5:14; 8:11), but there will be times when we inadvertently do something wrong, which the Spirit will make known to our conscience. Just because we've already been justified and forgiven through faith in Jesus Christ, we cannot simply ignore our wrongdoings, because our Father is holy and so cannot tolerate sin. But we can call upon the presence of our heavenly friend and advocate to come to our aid and restore a harmonious relationship with our Father.

As we confess and admit our wrongdoing, Jesus stands alongside us, lending his righteous presence and sacrifice for sin to reconcile our spirits to God. Unlike my advocate friend, however, whom I promptly reimbursed, our heavenly advocate cannot be repaid. He offers his righteous sacrifice as a gift of grace: nothing we could do or say could ever earn or repay it. But we can show how much we honour his advocacy and appreciate his gift by ensuring we rid our lives of those things that are wrong—seeking to walk in the light of Christ as we keep in step with the Spirit (1 John 1:7; Galatians 5:25).

WHEN WE SIN WILFULLY

This is also true for the things we choose to do wrong, even though we know we shouldn't. According to the laws of this land, I've not committed murder, theft or any other such crime that warrants a legal penalty, so I've not yet had to call upon an advocate to represent me in court for a wilful offence. But as a Christian, my spiritual citizenship is now in heaven (Philippians 3:20), and I only have to begin to read Christ's kingdom teaching to know I fall far short of its standards (see, for example, Matthew 5:17—7:6).

Like Paul, 'in my inner being I delight in God's law' (Romans 7:22), but when I'm put to the test, the evidence of my impatient, unkind, critical or selfish attitudes goes against me. I do want to honour God with my life, but I recognise that I continue to fall short of his glory; that there are times when I continue to choose my way rather than his, to satisfy my cravings rather than God's pleasure, to uphold my reputation rather than the honour of my king. And for that, as for my unintentional sins, I have need of a heavenly advocate to acknowledge my guilt and restore my broken unity with God.

WHEN WE ARE ACCUSED FALSELY

It's not just when we plead guilty that we have need of an advocate; he also comes to our defence when we're innocent, pleading our cause if we're falsely accused.

I would like to say that the innocent are always justified, but many a time the wicked find loopholes to win their legal battles in law courts, run roughshod over broken families, or feed their unending greed to the detriment of others. Indeed, although we hope for the perfection of eternal life with God, we continue to suffer the ravages of our enemy's characteristics permeating life in this fallen world: hardship, pain, rejection, injustice and even martyrdom at the hands of those who have yet to bow the knee to Christ as Lord.

But we have an advocate on high who understands adversity. Only Jesus will ever be called 'the Righteous One', and yet 'he was oppressed and afflicted… by oppression and judgment he was taken away' and 'assigned a grave with the wicked', even though he had done no wrong (Isaiah 53:7–9). In fact, 'The chief priests and the whole Sanhedrin were looking for false evidence against Jesus so that they could put him to death' (Matthew 26:59).

Jesus understands how it feels to be falsely accused. Moreover, no matter what evil is perpetrated against us in this world, our heavenly advocate stands before the Father in our defence, clothing us in his righteousness in a kingdom where the enemy has no influence.

So if, like me, you are suffering the consequences of injustice, take time out to meditate on Psalm 37 and focus your heart—not on the pain, unfairness and wickedness of the ways of the god of this world, but on your righteous advocate who stands alongside you, stating your cause before your Father in heaven.

Wickedness may get its way for a time and cause us great suffering, but its perpetrators shall one day join us in bowing the knee to King Jesus; and on that day, our righteousness in Christ will shine like the noonday sun, for the arrogant cannot stand in God's presence and their deceitful schemes will be shown for what they are. Our suffering is temporary, but our hope for justice is assured in eternity.

Meanwhile, we are not to fret or smoulder with anger,

jealousy and resentment when the wicked always seem to get their own way. Rather, we are to delight ourselves in our knowledge of and relationship with God, commit ourselves in trusting obedience to his ways, and wait patiently for his deliverance from evil, be that in this world or in the next.

So let's give thanks that, as we confess our own sins, our advocate will continue to act on our behalf in heaven, thereby maintaining the close relationship we can have with God our Father, which will sustain us, no matter what we go through in this world. Indeed, 'Do not fret because of evil men or be envious of those who do wrong; for like the grass they will soon wither, like green plants they will soon die away. Trust in the Lord and do good' (Psalm 37:1–3a).

TAKE IT FURTHER

Reflect

John said he wrote his letter 'so that you will not sin' (1 John 2:1). Sin doesn't just unsettle our peace with God; it grieves his Spirit intensely (Ephesians 4:30). When my daughter did something wrong, I may have felt frustrated, I may have grown impatient, I may even have got really cross at times; but overriding all those emotions was a sense of sadness that she didn't respect the way we'd taught her to live. Our heavenly Father has given his word to teach us his ways and his Spirit to guide our response. Are we grieving him by shunning his characteristics and choosing our own preferred lifestyle?

Pray

'Search me, O God, and know my heart; test me and know my anxious thoughts. See if there is any offensive way in me, and lead me in the way everlasting.' (Psalm 139:23–24)

Read

1 John 1:5—2:17; Ephesians 4:17—5:21; Psalm 37

JESUS:
THE ALPHA AND THE OMEGA

New Year's resolutions may well accompany Big Ben chiming out an old year and heralding the new. But no matter the aspirations we have on 1 January, some, if not many, of the circumstances filling the next 365 days prove to be outside of our control.

Job loss, accident, rejection, storm damage, ill health or bereavement are just a few of the unplanned events that might sadly affect our good intentions or mapped-out goals. And while some of us anticipate the future with great excitement, others feel disillusioned and discouraged by previous anticipations that fell foul of unplanned upheaval. Some may even face the future with fear and trepidation, wondering if things can possibly get any worse.

So if, like me, certain events of the past twelve months have undermined your expectancy for the months to come, then pause to drink deeply of the awesome truth available to us in Jesus, who says, 'I am the Alpha and the Omega, the First and the Last, the Beginning and the End' (Revelation 22:13).

'Alpha' and 'omega' are the first and last letters of the

Greek alphabet. God exists outside of time: he was before the world that he created and will outlast it; he is the source and the goal of life. He is the first and last, the beginning and end of history itself—history that includes the lives of you and of me. And Jesus Christ, the resurrected, living Son of God, revealed himself to the apostle John, sharing and applying his Father's titles to himself, as only he can.

My times are in your hands… All the days ordained for me were written in your book before one of them came to be. (Psalm 31:15; 139:16)

I enjoy vegetable gardening and, when we moved to the manse, I hired a rota-tiller and ploughed up a third of our long stretch of lawn. Winter frosts helped to break down sticky clumps of clay. Digging it over cleaned the patch of unwanted stones, but I still had to wait a number of months for the right season for planting, so I used that time productively to plan it.

I decided what I wanted to grow and where, taking into account the special needs of certain plants for sun or shade, then worked out the different sowing and harvest cycles to make best use of the garden.

Eventually, the time came for the first seed to be carefully sown in composted drills, one type after another. But I didn't just abandon those seeds, seedlings and plants to their own devices. I watched them, nurtured them, watered them, sprayed them, fed them—and yes, I admit that from time to time I talked to them!

When it got too hot and the ground baked hard, I was

constantly out with my watering can. When the storms hit and the wind threatened, I was propping the plants up with canes. When disease struck, I cared for them, according to their need. But I never gave up on seeing them through the season to encourage those seeds to fulfil their potential and harvest the crops they'd been chosen for.

Now I hope this doesn't sound too twee, but isn't that a picture of the master of our lives—the one who knows and determines the beginning and the end of life in this world?

It was he who chose us before creation, that we may know and love him (Ephesians 1:4). It was he who designed the heavens and the earth as a suitable place in which we could live (Genesis 1). It was he who prepared in advance the works that we would do in order to produce the fruit he wished us to bear (Ephesians 2:10). And it was he who determined the time and place in which each of us would live (Acts 17:26).

Furthermore, we are promised that Christ will always be with us (Matthew 28:20), that God will never leave or abandon us (Hebrews 13:5). He is the First and the Last, but he will also be with us at the centre of life's ups and downs, if we choose to let him.

Many are the plans in a human heart, but it is the Lord's purpose that prevails. (Proverbs 19:21)

Of course, it's easy to say or write these truths in theory, but if we're stepping into the future burdened with uncertainty, perhaps it's an appropriate moment to reflect on how well we engage with them in practice.

Four years ago, I sensed I should leave paid employment

to focus on my work as a freelance writer. My husband and I trusted God to provide for our needs, and we believe we've been good stewards, but that trust and careful budgeting were severely challenged when we recently experienced an unexpected financial need—one that was impossible to meet from our limited resources.

My trust and dependency were further challenged 36 hours later when, as a result of God's impeccable timing, I happened upon an ideal opportunity to take a second job, which would enable us to meet this financial need.

But as grateful and amazed as we were at God's provision, I hate to admit that I resented this unexpected intrusion into the life and work I'd grown to cherish, which provided such personal pleasure and fulfilment.

A couple of weeks went by as various arrangements were put in place, during which time the Lord tended me gently, pruned off a few unhelpful appendages to my life and disciplined my attitudes.

Fully surrendered and bowled over by his grace, I was ready to adapt and take on the second job. But, the very night before I was due to start, yet another unexpected event shook up my organised, tidy life, so much so that I felt as if I'd been turned upside down—my prearranged, compartmentalised 'plans' mixed up and shaken out into a disorganised heap on the floor.

Within a couple of days, I was flying to Guernsey to be with my family as we grieved for the untimely death of my brother.

Our circumstances may not be exactly as we would have chosen, expected or anticipated. We may not have the material wealth we'd like, we may not be part of certain relationships we hoped for, we may not feel as fulfilled in our work or social environments as we'd originally thought we would be; but, if we believe scripture, then we have absolute assurance that our days are in God's eternal hands, that they are planned and purposed by him whose thoughts and ways are far higher than our own, and we have a hope for the future that is 'an anchor for the soul, firm and secure' (Hebrews 6:19).

That's not to say we don't make plans or pursue relationships and activities that we believe are meaningful and helpful, will glorify God and might ultimately bring us happiness. But unless we keep these pursuits in perspective with the true source and goal of life—the knowledge of the Alpha and the Omega—we shall certainly fall prey to feelings of confusion, bitterness, dismay, pessimism, fear, loneliness and so on, as some aspects of life don't turn out as we'd anticipated or hoped.

I can truly say as I sit here writing, waiting for my brother's funeral, that the presence of the Alpha and the Omega has propped me up, watered and fed me, spoken tenderly to my heart and simply been with me. I don't believe I've reached the end of my season, so there's still more fruit to bear.

We have this hope as an anchor for the soul, firm and secure. (Hebrews 6:19)

I may not be 'feeling' the happiness that I would choose, as I survey the remnants of shattered hopes and dreams, scattered across the path of my unpredictable life. But one thing I do know: God is with me. And, as David said, 'apart from [him] I have no good thing' (Psalm 16:2). Apart from the secure, faithful, protective, all-knowing, eternal, loving presence of Jesus, nothing in this life can compare—not money, not work, not dreams, nor even these precious yet fragile relationships that come and go through different stages of life.

In Christ alone we find completeness, wholeness and purpose in life. Sometimes it will glow with the pleasure of happy, fulfilling, comforting circumstances; but sometimes it will take us through cold, shady valleys, knowing only that the Lord is with us. He takes hold of our hand and says, 'Do not fear; I will help you' (Isaiah 41:13).

So, wherever you are in life at the moment, be confident of this, 'that he who began a good work in you will carry it on to completion until the day of Christ Jesus' (Philippians 1:6).

TAKE IT FURTHER

Reflect

Happiness gained from pleasure, success and right relationships in this world is temporary and often fickle; but we can know Christ's joy (John 15:11) as we keep our hearts focused on the true source of life, as we live with increasing dependence on his presence in every part of life, and as we set our sights on the joy that awaits us, living with him for eternity.

Pray

'Whoever believes in me, as the Scripture has said, will have streams of living water flowing from within.' (John 7:38)

Lord Jesus, you are the source of my life. You are the only goal worth pursuing. May your rivers of living water flow out of my heart to nourish and to bless others along the path of life you've chosen for me.

Read

Revelation 22:12–17; Psalm 32; Isaiah 55:6–13

JESUS:
THE AMEN

Relationships can be a fabulous source of companionship, support, fun, guidance, equipping, intimacy, encouragement and much more. Sadly, however, the people with whom we are in relationship may own a 'title' that suggests one thing but they behave in quite the opposite manner.

Perhaps even today, some of us are suffering the consequences of a person who has not followed through on their purported character, identity or role: a close friend now behaving like an enemy, a husband who has broken his marriage vows, an adviser whose poor counsel has been detrimental to our livelihood, a teacher who has taught us incorrectly, a father who has abused or misused parental love, a provider who has abandoned us to our own limited resources, a helper who has left us to our inadequate devices, a team that has rejected us from their company, a health professional who has misdiagnosed our need for healing, a Christian behaving in contradiction to God's truth.

Sadly, we all get let down in our relationships to one degree or another, for no one is perfect. But there is one relationship offered to all of us that will never, ever let us down—our relationship with Jesus.

The different scriptural names or titles used of Jesus describe or identify his divine person, character, authority, ability and roles, and we are invited to relate to him an all these aspects.

We turn now to his title, 'The Amen', with which he introduced himself to the church in Laodicea (Revelation 3:14). It's a title he adopted from his Father, referring to God's sovereignty undergirding this world's events. (See Isaiah 65:16: your English translation may read 'the God of truth', which in Hebrew is literally 'the God of amen').

In prayer, of course, 'amen' is very familiar. It stems from a Hebrew word that signifies something certain, accurate, trustworthy and loyal. And so we still say 'amen' to validate that what is being prayed is true, that we accept and affirm it, or to indicate our hope for the prayer to be fulfilled.

Jesus often used the word 'amen' at the beginning rather than the end of a sentence, to accentuate the truth of what he was about to say: the word is often translated in our English Bibles as 'I tell you the truth…' (see, for example, Matthew 5:18). In so doing, Jesus affirmed the divine authority of what he was about to say.

And so, when Jesus used the word as a personal designation, he identified himself as the source of unwavering confidence in what was being said, prayed or proclaimed. Jesus—the Amen—is unchanging in his faithfulness and expresses the unchangeable truth of God's promises. He is steadfast in all he is, all he says and all he does: 'For no matter how many promises God has made, they are 'Yes' in Christ' (2 Corinthians 1:20).

With that in mind, it may be helpful to survey all the

names and attributes of Jesus that we will consider in this book: our Advocate, the Alpha and the Omega, the Apostle, the Author, the Bread of Life, the Door, the Faithful Witness, the Good Shepherd, the Head of the Church, the Holy One, our Hope, our Husband, I Am, the Image of the Invisible God, King of Kings, the Lamb of God, the Life, the Light, the Living Stone, Prince of Peace, our Protector, the Resurrection and the Life, the Rock, Ruler of the Kings of the Earth, the Teacher, the True Vine, the Truth, the Way, the Wisdom of God, Wonderful Counsellor, and the Word of God (there are still more you may find and wish to reflect on in your personal Bible studies).

In all these identities, roles, character traits and capabilities, Jesus is perfectly trustworthy, for Jesus is 'the Amen'. But the extent to which we truly believe that will be proved by the extent to which we put our faith into practice, by whether our professed beliefs are actually being worked out in our lives.

Anyone can just say 'amen' to a prayer, but it may be harder to say it sincerely if the prayer expresses a personal response to God with acts of trust, dedication, surrender, vulnerability or sacrifice.

Moreover, it takes our whole heart, mind, soul and strength to kneel before our Lord Jesus and say with an open, surrendered heart, 'I believe—and I will consequently live out those beliefs in practice, in accordance with your ways and your will, even though I may not always understand the way you choose to do things.'

Jesus longs for us to renew our dependency on our relationship with him. We may recognise that we relate better to the people, pursuits and things of this world but, unlike them, Jesus will never let us down.

Jesus is ever faithful, ever true to all that he claims to be. So will we give him the response he is worthy to receive?

Praise the Lord. Praise, O servants of the Lord, praise the name of the Lord. Let the name of the Lord be praised, both now and forevermore. From the rising of the sun to the place where it sets, the name of the Lord is to be praised. (Psalm 113:1–3)

Amen? Amen!

TAKE IT FURTHER

What are you depending on?

Jesus called himself the Amen—expressing his unchanging faithfulness and truth—in contrast to the wavering church in Laodicea, who were reprimanded for being 'neither cold nor hot' (Revelation 3:15). In words they professed their belief in Christ, but in practice they depended on their wealth, expertise and success for security and fulfilment, and to guide their priorities as to what to do with their lives.

- Do you sincerely believe in Christ's unchanging faithfulness and truth?
- What kinds of things might be hindering you or distracting you from trusting Jesus and working out the commitment

to him that you profess with your lips? For example, your job, financial security, talents, hobbies, relationships, lifestyle, habits, obsessions, cravings, infatuations, opinions, fears, expectations, dreams…

Jesus said, 'Anyone who intends to come with me has to let me lead. You're not in the driver's seat—I am. Don't run from suffering; embrace it. Follow me and I'll show you how. Self-help is no help at all. Self-sacrifice is the way, my way, to finding yourself, your true self. What good would it do to get everything you want and lose you, the real you?' (Luke 9:23–24, THE MESSAGE)

What holds you back?

Take another look at the list of names and titles given to Jesus. Are there any that you still find difficult to trust, relate or surrender to?

- Look them up in context, in your Bible, and reflect on what the meaning implies for your relationship with Jesus.
- Talk to a Christian friend if you're struggling to understand what it means or how you might need to respond. Ask your friend to pray with you.
- Ask Jesus to open your heart to his perfect love and purpose, which abounds in every facet of his nature, character and purpose—encompassed by the 'Amen' in every title that he bears.

'You are to give him the name Jesus, because he will save his people from their sins.' (Matthew 1:21)

'He has sent me to bind up the brokenhearted, to proclaim free-dom for the captives and release from darkness for the prisoners, to proclaim the year of the Lord's favour and the day of vengeance of our God, to comfort all who mourn, and provide for those who grieve in Zion—to bestow on them a crown of beauty instead of ashes, the oil of gladness instead of mourning, and a garment of praise instead of a spirit of despair.' (Isaiah 61:1–3)

Can you truthfully say 'amen'?

When you say 'amen' to a prayer:

- Do you simply say it out of routine or tradition?
- Or do you say it only when you can identify completely with the praise, surrender, hopes, goals, lifestyle and pur-pose expressed through the prayer in relation to Christ's divine truth, faithfulness and authority?

Guard your steps when you go to the house of God. Go near to listen, rather than to offer the sacrifice of fools, who do not know that they do wrong. Do not be quick with your mouth, do not be hasty in your heart to utter anything before God. God is in heaven and you are on earth, so let your words be few. As a dream comes when there are many cares, so the speech of a fool when there are many words. When you make a vow to God, do not delay in fulfilling it. He has no pleasure in fools; fulfil your vow. It is better not to vow than to make a vow and not fulfil it. Do not let your mouth lead you into sin… Therefore stand in awe of God. (Ecclesiastes 5:1–7)

JESUS:
THE APOSTLE

Have you ever been sent off to do something, but went feeling nothing but inadequacy and despair, knowing you didn't have a clue how to do it?

If I was sent outside to fix the boss's car, I certainly wouldn't know where to start, unless a car mechanic accompanied me. Even something seemingly simple like retrieving an item from a high shelf is impossible for someone as short as me, unless a taller person is present.

It's the ability to fulfil a task or a role, on the basis that we're sent in the company of someone who can do it, that we're reflecting on in this chapter.

Only once in scripture is Jesus called 'the apostle' (Hebrews 3:1); it's a name or office that may be more familiar to us in terms of his followers. But when the writer to the Hebrews used this title, it reaffirmed that Jesus was sent by God to accomplish his purpose of salvation.

This is what 'apostle' means in the Greek: 'one who is sent'.

Jesus said, 'My food is to do the will of him who sent me and to finish his work… For I have come down from heaven not to do my will but to do the will of him who sent me…

I do nothing on my own but speak just what the Father has taught me' (John 4:34; 6:38; 8:28).

Jesus claimed to be an apostle—'sent' to accomplish God's will—and he proved it in practice as his ministry was accompanied by the signs, wonders and miracles that distinguish an apostle (2 Corinthians 12:12). And yet he made one thing very clear: 'By myself I can do nothing,' he said (John 5:30), but 'the very work that the Father has given me to finish, and which I am doing, testifies that the Father has sent me' (v. 36).

Jesus could not minister with supernatural power unless he was accompanied by the one who would enable him to do so, the one whose presence enriched the flesh of a man with the divine power of God. These supernatural happenings did not prove Christ's divinity. He was divine from conception and refused to provide signs to people who would not first believe in his person (Matthew 12:38–39; Mark 8:11–12).

Nevertheless, the signs, wonders and miracles are the supernatural consequence—the resultant outworking of the divine—in one who has been sent in the power and presence of God to reveal his infinite love for humankind, to rescue them from their imprisonment in Satan's dominion of death, and to reconcile them to their Creator.

Furthermore, Jesus sent out his own representatives to assist him in fulfilling God's work—twelve men who spent three years in the intimate presence of Jesus; eating, sleeping, walking, talking and living with the Son of God. Technically, these apostles died out after the first century, but that doesn't mean Jesus no longer needs them. In fact, he continues to appoint and send out apostles to reflect God's love and proclaim his message of reconciliation, accompanied by the presence and empowering of the Spirit.

Indeed, it was only because Jesus accomplished God's plan of salvation through his perfect life, death and resurrection that we can be reconciled to God, and so enjoy his presence and empowering as Jesus did. It was only because he first fulfilled his role as the apostle of God that others can become apostles too.

And so, just before he died, Jesus prayed, 'As you sent me into the world, I have sent them into the world' (John 17:18), thereby passing the 'apostleship baton' on to his disciples.

They, in turn, passed it down through the centuries and now it's been handed to us—sent out in the power of God to make known to the world that Jesus is the only way the imprisoned can be set free and imbued with spiritual life. And if we're moving in the will and the ways of God, then we can expect to see the marks of apostleship, the supernatural signs, wonders and miracles bearing witness to the source of our work.

Together, we have become Christ's living body, through which he continues his ministry in the world—individuals who are dependent on one another to accomplish God's purpose in full.

Consequently, Paul teaches that the empowering of the Holy Spirit is given in different ways to different people (Romans 12:6; 1 Corinthians 12:11), and for some there is a spiritually empowered ministry of apostleship (1 Corinthians 12:28–29; Ephesians 4:11), emphasising missionary work and church-building. Nevertheless, he has sent all of us, not some of us, into the world to share and proclaim the love and relationship we have with God.

Maybe, however, we feel too spiritually unfit to take our turn at running with the apostleship baton in this particular 'relay race'. Or perhaps we're trying, but we keep stumbling, falling or dropping the baton.

If so, be encouraged, because all athletes need to train first. The apostles only fulfilled their role because they were first trained by *the* Apostle, and we can take some training tips too. As Paul says, 'Everyone who competes in the games goes into strict training. They do it to get a crown that will not last; but we do it to get a crown that will last forever' (1 Corinthians 9:25). And the writer to the Hebrews adds, 'Therefore… let us run with perseverance the race marked out for us' (Hebrews 12:1).

TRAINING TIPS FOR RUNNING WITH THE 'APOSTLESHIP BATON'

First, stop. Take regular time to simply enjoy being with Jesus. It's essential we take time regularly to enjoy being in Christ's presence. Of course, Jesus is with us constantly through his Spirit, but it is only when we stop, listen, worship, pray and reflect on his word to our hearts—when we just make space to 'be' who we are with him—that we, like the disciples, may begin to really know him and be inspired by him.

How else can we share the love of God, unless we've first

experienced it for ourselves? How can we teach about God unless we've known him ourselves, or manifest the power of God unless we've experienced it ourselves?

'Who will devote himself to be close to me?' declares the Lord. (Jeremiah 30:21)

'Come with me by yourselves to a quiet place and get some rest.' (Mark 6:31)

Be still, and know that I am God. (Psalm 46:10)

'Call to me and I will answer you and tell you great and unsearchable things you do not know.' (Jeremiah 33:3)

Second, ditch self-effort and expect to be empowered supernaturally. Jesus lived and moved in the fullness of God's power because he did only what God wanted him to do. This was the result of following the first training tip—spending considerable time in private prayer with his heavenly Father.

He got up very early to pray, while it was still dark (Mark 1:35). He often withdrew alone to pray (Luke 5:16) and went up mountainsides to spend whole nights in prayer (6:12). As a result, he knew where and when he should minister (see tip 3 below) and did so accompanied by signs, wonders and miracles (Mark 1:35–42).

As we first seek God in prayer, his divine empowering is the natural (or, should I say, supernatural) consequence, flowing through our lives. Do you rely on your own capability or the power of his presence to empower your tasks?

Jesus once went up a mountainside to pray, the result of which was the glorious transfiguration (Luke 9:28–29)! What might God do in and through your life as you simply spend time in his presence?

'In him we live, and move, and have our being.' (Acts 17:28)

Third, don't run aimlessly (1 Corinthians 9:26) but know where you are sent.

'Therefore go and make disciples of all nations, baptising them in the name of the Father and of the Son and of the Holy Spirit, and teaching them to obey everything I have commanded you… You will receive power when the Holy Spirit comes on you; and you will be my witnesses in Jerusalem, and in all Judea and Samaria, and to the ends of the earth.' (Matthew 28:19–20; Acts 1:8)

No individual can meet every person or visit every country, but each of us has been sent to the people in our generation with the ongoing challenge to be Christ's apostles—to our families, colleagues, communities and so on.

Do you perceive your routines as the mere consequence of life so far or as part of God's predetermined plan to reach all peoples in every place and generation?

How are you fulfilling your unique apostleship as part of his divine purpose?

We are God's workmanship, created in Christ Jesus to do good works, which God prepared in advance for us to do. (Ephesians 2:10)

'Go! I am sending you out like lambs among wolves… I have given you authority to trample on snakes and scorpions and to overcome all the power of the enemy; nothing will harm you.' (Luke 10:3, 19)

JESUS:
THE AUTHOR

Authors create, and in so doing they invite readers into the experience of their creation, guiding them from a chosen starting point to a predetermined end. The reader may or may not enjoy the journey; may or may not agree with the author's opinions; may even put the book down and imagine their own scenario to continue or conclude the plot. But ultimately, the book is the author's creation, and only he or she has authority to determine its structure and detail.

In fact, the word 'author' is not bound to the creation of books but can be used to describe a founder (of a city or school, for example) or the source of an atmosphere (of peace or terror...). In its simplest meaning, as translated from ancient Greek, an author may also be a leader, ruler or chief (Acts 5:31, translated 'Prince' in the NIV).

When we turn to scripture, we find Jesus described as 'author' on a number of occasions.

THE AUTHOR OF LIFE (ACTS 3:15)

Acts 3 records how Peter and John were used by God to heal a crippled beggar at the temple gate in Jerusalem. It's not surprising that an amazed crowd gathered around them, but Peter responded, 'You disowned the Holy and Righteous One and asked that a murderer be released to you. You killed the author of life, but God raised him from the dead' (Acts 3:14–15).

When I picture the beggar holding on to the apostle, facing the crowd, I can't help but imagine Peter with a bemused smile as he depicts the irony of the situation. Many people had sought to meddle with Jesus' life and message, to the extreme of trying to kill him, and yet the exact opposite had happened. It is absurd to think that anyone could kill the author—the source—of everlasting life!

There are people today, however, who still try to meddle with Jesus, who attempt to shout him down, mock his claims, belittle his opinions and turn their backs on what he has to offer. Nevertheless, he continues to reach out to the world so that all may experience his gift of spiritual life. This isn't just something to hope for patiently, once our physical body dies; it is a life that we can begin to experience now in all the fullness, purpose and power of Christ himself.

But just as we can choose which books we want to read and ignore the ones we're not interested in, we're also given a choice as to whether or not we accept the words of the author of life and what he wants to give us.

Have you dismissed the source of everlasting spiritual life, satisfied with trying to make the best of the few years of physical life we each have on this earth? Or are you hungry for more, and willing to take the author at his word, accepting his free gift of eternal life with God your heavenly Father?

Through him all things were made; without him nothing was made that has been made. In him was life, and that life was the light of all people. The light shines in the darkness, but the darkness has not understood it. (John 1:3–5)

THE AUTHOR OF SALVATION (HEBREWS 2:10)

In simple terms, a book comprises a beginning, middle and end. Just as a book wouldn't be a book if it only had an introduction, so Jesus—the author of salvation—doesn't just provide the source of spiritual life. He leads us into its subsequent outworking as he guides us in his predetermined ways—ways that make us holy (Hebrews 2:10–11).

The word 'salvation' refers to the means of both rescuing and preserving something from harm. And so Jesus, who is the means by which we are rescued from spiritual death, doesn't abandon us until we meet him in heaven, but protects and preserves our spiritual life as he leads us in his holy ways.

Jesus engaged with the limitations, joys and sufferings of human life so that we might know about eternal life, but it's only as we allow the author of salvation to lead us into his own higher experience that we can engage with our spiritual life in full measure.

As we allow the author to guide us in his ways of salvation, we receive spiritual protection from the enemy who seeks to harm us or limit our effectiveness in this temporary, tangible world. Furthermore, the essence of Jesus will be expressed through our life and, consequently, 'read' and experienced by others.

We cannot earn salvation, but, as we align ourselves to its author through the life of the Spirit of Christ within, our spiritual life will develop and be used in accordance with God's perfect purpose.

Therefore, my dear friends, as you have always obeyed... continue to work out your salvation with fear and trembling, for it is God who works in you to will and to act according to his good purpose. (Philippians 2:12–13)

THE AUTHOR AND FINISHER OF OUR FAITH (HEBREWS 12:2)

When I get bored or disinterested in a book, I sometimes set it aside without ever reaching the end. Life too can, at times, feel boring, confusing or just so difficult that we're tempted to abandon Christ's intentions and try to live it our way. But the author has already completed the story of life lived by faith, and encourages us to persevere to its end.

Jesus is both the beginning and the end of a spiritual life of faith. (The NIV uses the word 'perfecter' in Hebrews 12:2.) Furthermore, he lived that life in a physical body without compromise, denial or any hint of giving up—a tremendous encouragement when we feel overwhelmed by the world, which may sometimes divert us from God's intentions.

The author and finisher of our faith possibly lost his father Joseph fairly early in life; he was brought up in near poverty and, at first, as a refugee. His adult claims were initially rejected by his own family and community, and he didn't have a home, so he relied on the kindness of others' hospitality, which probably wasn't available each and every day of his three-year public ministry.

He was pressured by people's expectations, assailed by demonic temptation to transfer his allegiance from God, scorned by religious leaders, inundated by growing crowds seeking his miraculous powers, deserted by his closest friends, falsely accused and whipped almost to death. He had his hair pulled out, he was punched, kicked and tortured with thorns, and he finished his physical life accompanied by the indescribable suffering of crucifixion.

Indeed, the author of the life of salvation that we are working out in this world knows how it feels when we're tempted to 'close the book'! But he went ahead and trod the path of faith himself, first to procure eternal life on our behalf but also to encourage us to overcome physical obstacles as we keep our focus on him (Hebrews 12:1–2). Therefore, 'Consider him who endured such opposition from sinners, so that you will not grow weary and lose heart' (Hebrews 12:3). Consider, too, that Jesus doesn't just encourage us from a distance but also works in us by his Holy Spirit, equipping us with everything good for doing what is pleasing to him (Hebrews 13:21).

The author of life began a new thing when he was made in human likeness—a perfect work that permitted others to enter into his own experience of relationship with God and to receive its spiritual blessings. So let's not just accept him but let's also surrender to the way that the author wants to lead us through this life, keeping focused on him and not on the circumstances surrounding us or the distraction of how we might prefer the story to be written. As we do so, we can rest assured that he will lead us safely through the concluding chapter of life in this world and onwards into the never-ending story of our eternal life with God.

TAKE IT FURTHER

Reflect

Do we accept the author's predetermined plan for our life, and do we surrender to his guidance through it?

Do we attempt to embellish his plans with our own opinions of how the life of faith should be worked out or are we humbly submitting to his word?

Do we fear the difficult parts of the story, or even the end? If so, take time to talk to the author about it and trust that he will never leave us at those times, but will encourage, equip and be with us every step of the way.

Pray

Lord Jesus, I find great comfort knowing that you have already walked this path of life before me and know the end from its beginning. Thank you that nothing will surprise you, but in all circumstances you will show me which way to turn, as I keep my focus on you. Amen

Read

Acts 3:1–26; Hebrews 2:9–15; Hebrews 12:1–17; 2 Peter 1:3–11

JESUS:
THE BREAD OF LIFE

Bread is one of the oldest foods known to have been prepared by people, possibly dating back to prehistoric times. It's been part of our basic diet for thousands of years. Admittedly, folk suffering with gluten or yeast allergies have to be careful what type of bread they eat but, for most of us, the health benefits of vital nutrients found in wholegrain bread remain undisputed; they can reduce the risk of heart attack or relieve constipation, for example, and eating a slice of bread at bedtime may even alleviate insomnia.

It's poignant, therefore, that Jesus called himself 'the bread of life' (John 6:35). At the time, he was walking on the northern shore of the Sea of Galilee, having just arrived in the fishing town of Capernaum (vv. 16–24).

Astounded by the previous day's miracle on the mountainside (vv. 1–14), the Galileans were eager to see Jesus again—the man who could heal the sick with a mere word or touch and, with a simple prayer of thanks, could multiply five small loaves and two small fish into the gargantuan quantity required to satisfy 5000 hungry tummies. Times were harsh while they lived under Roman rule, but surely this man had sufficient power to lead them against their oppressors? Here was a potential king who would provide for their needs and under whom they could live at ease. And so, 'they got into the boats and went to Capernaum in search of Jesus' (v. 24).

The trouble was, the Galileans were motivated by what they perceived as the promise of an easy life: political independence, the eradication of debilitating or life-threatening illness, and all their physical needs simply handed to them on a plate... or in a basket! It certainly sounds like a good life to me, if that's all that life consists of, but Jesus came to give life to the full (John 10:10)—fullness made possible only when our physical life dovetails with our spiritual life; when our short-lived, temporary life walks hand-in-hand with that which will last for ever.

So what stirs our hearts to search for Jesus—to take time and effort to escape the treadmill of life for a while and meet with him? We need only take a look at our list of prayer requests, be they written on our hearts or on paper, to ascertain our primary motive for seeking the Lord. But as much as scripture encourages us to pray about our problems, governments and situations in the world, Jesus reminds us that, first and foremost, he wants us to come to him to nourish our souls.

UNDERSTANDING THE IMAGE

Bread was a staple food of the Israelites' diet—not the choice of white, wholemeal, seeded, sliced, large, small, Italian, French, farmhouse or gluten-free options that we now enjoy in the West, but, nevertheless, a cultural equivalent that met their bodies' requirement for physical sustenance.

Bodies, after all, need food in order to live; the fact that we were created with a fundamental need for sustenance reiterates our dependency on our Creator to provide it. And so, moved with compassion for the hungry crowds up the mountainside, Jesus proved his relationship with the Creator when he provided for their need in a way that the Galileans could never have asked or imagined (John 6:5–13).

But Jesus didn't come to impart a supernatural miracle as the answer to every problem in life. He came with a far greater purpose—to save our souls from spiritual death. That's why John calls these miracles 'signs': physical evidence of Christ's deity, which in turn supported his messianic claims that would meet our deeper spiritual requirements.

Sadly, however, the Galileans were too engrossed with the physical needs of life to perceive any spiritual hunger and, consequently, misread his sign. All they could see was the potential of a powerful leader and provider. They believed in his abilities but failed to believe in his person, and so Jesus challenged their motives for seeking him. Calling himself 'the bread of life', he offered inward satisfaction that work cannot earn or money buy—spiritual life, strength and wholeness, in this world and the next.

'I am the living bread that came down from heaven. Whoever eats of this bread will live for ever' (v. 51). Many of the Galileans turned their backs on him, hungry for the material but lacking any spiritual appetite for forgiveness and eternal life—a decision we all have to make. If you've not yet accepted Jesus as your Lord, then please reread his words, for only he can breathe eternal life into your spirit.

ARE YOU DISILLUSIONED?

Even as Christian believers, the difficulties we face can easily overshadow our need to continue feeding our spirits on the 'bread of life', our natural appetite overwhelming any sense of a spiritual appetite. But Jesus knew that our ongoing spiritual needs were, and are, just as real and important as our physical needs. As we seek him to satisfy them, we receive inward strength, comfort, peace and vigour to cope with life in the world.

It is true that one should feed the starving stomachs of the poor, homeless or refugees before offering them spiritual fodder, but, for those of us already well-fed, we can become so engrossed in our many tangible needs and desires that we lose sight of our ever-present spiritual needs. Indeed, our need of Jesus to provide spiritual bread is no less real than our need for physical bread if we want to experience an abiding relationship with him (v. 56).

Jesus knows that we need food, warmth, clothing and shelter to exist, but some of us may feel that he's failed to meet our needs as we'd wanted or expected. We may have once been impressed by the stories we heard about his timely, ingenious provision, only to find that he doesn't provide all our wants quite in the way that we'd hoped.

Such disappointment can cause a tragic sense of disillusionment in the person and promises of Christ if, like the Galileans, we've misunderstood his meaning. But again, Jesus reminds us, 'I am the bread of life. Whoever comes to me will never go hungry, and whoever believes in me will never be thirsty' (John 6:35).

With the recent downturn in the economy, the fallibility of financial savings and the ever-increasing threat of job loss, we might understandably lie awake at night, worrying about where the next meal or rent payment will come from. But while modern-day credit crises have undermined our physical security, they certainly haven't undermined or changed God's promises: 'Do not worry about your life, what you will eat or drink; or about your body, what you will wear. Is not life more important than food, and the body more important than clothes?' (Matthew 6:25).

This is not just a 'feel-good-factor' suggestion; it's a command to trust our lives into the hands of the only person who is completely trustworthy. 'Look at the birds of the air; they do not sow or reap or store away in barns, and yet your heavenly Father feeds them. Are you not much more valuable than they?' (v. 26).

ARE YOU HUNGRY?

When I start feeling light-headed and irritable, it's a sure sign I've been working too long and am overdue for a meal. Perhaps you suffer in similar fashion when your body is running low on fuel, or maybe headache and lethargy are your telltale symptoms.

But when we feel unsettled or stressed, lacking inner peace and the comfort or strength of God's presence, I wonder how often we recognise it as a sign that we're overdue a spiritual meal. We may have become so anxious, busy or distracted that we've not spent adequate time nourishing our souls with

Jesus, feeding on God's word and listening to him in prayer.

Indeed, bread continues to be a staple dietary requirement. Some would shun its sustenance in the pursuit of a
'size-zero' figure, but experts reiterate the benefits of eating
it. Let's not permit current trends of diet, disillusionment or
busy routines to distract us from feeding both body and soul
in an appropriate, nourishing way.

TAKE IT FURTHER

Reflect

Do we believe in Christ as our Lord and Saviour? If so, is our
faith for eternal life based on that future or merely on Christ's
ability to relieve us of difficult situations now?

How well are we feeding both our physical and spiritual
lives? If one side is better fed than the other, how might we
redress the balance?

Pray

*Lord Jesus, forgive me when I've failed to feed my spirit in my zeal
to feed my body, my bank account, my hopes and dreams. I have
many 'wants' in life, but I recognise that only you can satisfy my
deepest needs. Please help me to recognise just what they are.*

Read

John 6:1–71; Philippians 3:7–11

JESUS:

THE DOOR INTO THE KINGDOM OF GOD

Almost 2000 years ago, beneath the darkened skies of Jerusalem, Jesus cried out from the horrors of crucifixion, then breathed his last dying breath. 'At that moment the curtain of the temple was torn in two from top to bottom' (Matthew 27:51).

This temple was famous for its fine architecture, exquisite furnishings and golden, bejewelled interior. Moreover, it enclosed the house of God—the Most Holy Place of his glorious presence among his people, veiled from view by a heavy, embroidered curtain. In fact, God's presence was inaccessible to anyone but the high priest and, even then, just once a year when he offered the blood of sacrifice to seek God's forgiveness on behalf of the people of Israel—a sacrifice that had to be made over and over again.

I can't help but wonder how shocked and bewildered the priests must have been as an unseen hand tore through the barrier to God's spiritual dwelling. But that incredible moment broadcast the fulfilment of Jesus' mission, opening the way for everyone—man, woman, Jew and Gentile—to enter God's presence themselves through the once-for-all, perfect sacrifice of Christ's life.

'I am the door,' Jesus says (ESV, translated 'gate' in the NIV); 'whoever enters through me will be saved' (John 10:9). As we journey through life, we come across various 'doors' of opportunity, some of which we choose to walk through (a new job, relationship, home, experience and so on) and some of which we choose to pass by. But in calling himself 'the door', Jesus offers the greatest opportunity of a lifetime.

Some of us may have already walked through this door, but, as we reflect on this image of Christ, I trust we'll be further equipped to point out the opportunity to others. Meanwhile, some of us may still be on the outside, contemplating Jesus, wondering what this door implies—and I pray that you will continue reading so that you may also be inspired to choose to walk on through.

Doors permit us to move from one place into another: from the outside to the inside, from the kitchen into the lounge, from the garage into the car. So let's consider why Christ applies this analogy to himself.

UNDERSTANDING THE IMAGE

We were all born into a physical world and, because we can use most, if not all, of our physical senses to see, hear, feel, taste or touch this tangible environment, we believe it to be 'real'. What may not be so easy to believe, however, is the existence of an unseen spiritual realm.

Physical life may tempt us into the sole pursuit of material comfort, wealth, promotion, self-satisfaction and so on, all of which are temporary. But Jesus offers life on a new dimension, empowered by his Spirit in the unseen realm both now and for eternity.

That's why Jesus calls himself 'the door'. If we pass through—that is, if we believe in him as the resurrected Son of God whose death became the perfect sacrifice for our sins—then we will walk into a new life, one enabling us to live in the security of an intimate relationship with God. Unless we choose to walk through 'the door', however, we shall never know God, neither in this physical life nor in the spiritual life that continues after death.

Prior to Jesus' life on earth, God was a distant authority, a stranger even to the temple priests who were bound by the Law of Moses. We read of a few men and women in the Old Testament who desired and grew to know God more deeply but who nevertheless relied upon relentless animal sacrifices to cleanse them of the sin that prevents intimacy with the Holy One.

When Jesus ministered on earth, however, he first showed us what God is like and then opened the way for us to know him for ourselves. But let's not be deceived: there is only one door to God and that is through belief in Jesus, who said, 'I am the way and the truth and the life. No one comes to the Father except through me' (John 14:6). Religious ritual, efforts to be good enough or a Christian heritage will never open the door to heaven.

UNPACKING THE MESSAGE

Are we experiencing God's kingdom?

Jesus said, 'The time has come. The kingdom of God is near. Repent and believe the good news!' (Mark 1:15).

Jesus represents more than a door into a belief system; he is the means of access into the awesome kingdom of God.

When we think about a kingdom or a kingship, we might perceive a geographical location ruled by a king. The kingdom of God, however, can't be found on a map but only by being established in believers' hearts as they put their trust in Christ and surrender to his kingship—his rule, reign and authority. And so the kingdom continues to grow through repentant, humble, devoted Christian lives whose eternal perspective far outweighs the temporary focus of worldly ideals. Difficulties and disappointments continue to hound us but the assurance of Christ's love, comfort, counsel, equipping and empowering strengthens us along life's path.

Have we submitted to Christ?

Jesus warned, 'Not everyone who says to me, "Lord, Lord," will enter the kingdom of heaven, but only those who do the will of my Father who is in heaven' (Matthew 7:21).

As we stand at the door of life and the gateway into God's kingdom—as we look upon the person of Christ—we each have an active response to make. We cannot do anything to earn the right to walk through the 'door', for Christ's sacrifice is a free gift that we just have to believe in and receive. Nevertheless, walking through the 'door' requires more than a mere declaration that Jesus is Lord; it seeks a genuine submission of the heart. Such surrender will be proved by the fruit that we bear—by our new priorities, attitudes, lifestyles, devotion, behaviour and so on, as we submit to the rule and reign of our king.

And so, as we walk through the 'door', we take personal responsibility to prove our faith by the deeds required of the kingdom of God (James 2:14–17), as we take time to read his word, listen to his voice in prayer and keep in step with the ways of his Spirit, who lives in the hearts of believers.

Are we still waiting at the door?

Jesus promised, 'Seek his kingdom, and these things will be given to you as well' (Luke 12:31).

There may yet be some readers still standing at the 'door', undecided as to what to do. Perhaps you're worried that submitting your life to Christ will result in the loss of relationships, career opportunities, financial security, the fulfilment of your lifelong dreams and even your reputation among family and friends. I cannot reassure you that none of these things will happen—although it's quite possible that none of them will.

Nevertheless, I can testify from personal experience that whatever our role in the kingdom of God may require, wherever it may take us, whatever our king may ask us to give up, take up or change—all of it, without exception, will be based on God's best and loving intentions. Furthermore, he'll provide everything we need, even if it's not everything we want.

God knew us before we were even born; he created us in our mother's womb and knew every day of our lives before one of them came to be (see Psalm 139). He is waiting, longing, for that glorious moment when each of us walk through the door of Christ into his kingdom, for therein awaits true life—life in all its fullness now, as the spiritual dovetails with the physical and the perfection of eternal life in the future.

'See, I have placed before you an open door that no one can shut' (Revelation 3:8). Choose for yourself this day, this moment, if you have faith to walk on through.

TAKE IT FURTHER

Reflect

For God so loved the world that he gave his one and only Son, that whoever believes in him shall not perish but have eternal life. (John 3:16)

Pray

Lord Jesus, I believe you know me already and have been waiting for this day. Here I am, wanting to walk through the door of your life, that I may live in the kingdom of God, both now and for eternity. Forgive me, Jesus, for walking independently of you all these years. I ask that you will wash me clean of the ungodly things that have upset and grieved you in my life. In faith, I now take hold of your loving hand, to walk with you and learn from you in surrender to your word and in the comfort of your presence at all times. Amen

(If you have prayed this prayer, please do make contact with a Christian friend or a local church where you may join with the family of God, learn together, serve together and find mutual support and encouragement.)

Read

Hebrews 10:19–22; Matthew 7:15–23; Luke 12:22–34

JESUS:
THE FAITHFUL WITNESS

A 'witness' is a person who has observed something or some-one and can therefore provide a testimony—an eyewitness account—of certain events, places or people. A person who 'bears' witness may themselves be the evidence of that which is being alleged. My skin, for example, which tans easily, bears witness to my Guernsey-Iberian ancestry.

The title 'faithful witness' was one that Jesus adopted both before and after his death and resurrection (John 8:14; Revelation 3:14), and John used it when writing the letter that we now call Revelation (1:5).

But Jesus was called a liar, a blasphemer and even the devil by those who did not believe in his teaching, his powers or his person. In fact, some of his contemporaries wanted to silence his verbal testimony and remove his visible wit-ness by seizing or even stoning him. So what was Jesus' witness, which caused such an uproar among so many of his contemporaries?

THE WITNESS TO GOD'S KINGDOM

The main thrust of Jesus' teaching centred on the coming of God's kingdom, and, while those to whom he spoke generally believed in God and heaven, not so many believed in his witness of it. In fact, relatively few believed that God's kingdom was being made available to them personally because of who Jesus claimed he was and the sacrifice he would ultimately make on their behalf.

From the tender age of twelve, and possibly earlier, Jesus called God his Father (Luke 2:49). Years later, he claimed that he alone had seen God (John 6:46) and affirmed that he was the Christ—the promised Messiah—who would bring salvation to Israel and, in turn, to the whole world (Matthew 16:16–17).

The Gospels provide numerous examples of Jesus' proficient teaching about God's kingdom—lessons and instructions displaying his expert knowledge and authority on the subject. His testimony was made possible only by the fact that he had witnessed it himself and expected to return once his work on earth was complete (John 8:57–59; 18:33–37).

THE WITNESS OF GOD

Jesus also bore witness to the nature of God. As God's Son, he bore his Father's likeness. As his life drew to a close, he declared how he had revealed God to the people and, later, Paul described him as being 'the image of the invisible God' (John 17:6; Colossians 1:15).

Jesus had been with his Father for all eternity (John 1:1), but spent time as a man on earth so that we might know the reality of God's character and being in action: his unconditional love, compassion, justice, mercy, righteousness, holiness, humour, tenderness, authority and power. As I've written elsewhere in this book, Christ revealed to his own generation and, through the Gospel witness, to all generations, the image of God whom no one has seen—the very essence of his nature, the perfect portrait of his character, the manifestation of his glory ('Jesus: the Image of the Invisible God, pp. 106–112). He was, and is, 'the radiance of God's glory and the exact representation of his being' (Hebrews 1:3).

THE WITNESS TO GOD'S WILL AND PURPOSE

Jesus only said what God wanted him to say and only did as he was told. In short, he was perfectly obedient in fulfilling his Father's purposes. 'I have come down from heaven not to do my will but to do the will of him who sent me,' he said (John 6:38; see also 12:49–50; 14:10). If the people were wondering what God was doing in first-century Palestine, they need only have looked to Jesus, who bore witness to it through his own work and ministry.

Indeed, by the end of his life, Jesus prayed, 'I have brought you glory on earth by completing the work you gave me to do' (John 17:4)—a work that was finally and perfectly completed on the cross when he cried out, 'It is finished' (19:30).

THE WITNESS TO THE WORLD

Although Jesus' task was completed, his witness to the world did not end when he ascended into heaven, but passed on to his disciples. 'You will receive power when the Holy Spirit comes on you', he said, 'and you will be my witnesses in Jerusalem, and in all Judea and Samaria, and to the ends of the earth' (Acts 1:8).

He didn't ask all of us to argue about God's existence or try to persuade others about the kingdom through intellectual debate, though some have been gifted in this area. He simply instructed us to witness to what we've experienced, just as he did.

Over the years, certain evangelists have encouraged my witness by reminding me that I have not been asked to take the role of a lawyer, as it were, and stand up in court to present my case in defence of God. I've simply been asked to sit in the witness box and provide an honest testimony of my personal experience, of the things I have witnessed in my life or in the lives of others. In so doing, I provide the necessary evidence of God's nature, kingdom and purpose, but after that it is up to the jury—those listening to my words or observing my actions—to decide for themselves if they believe my testimony is true.

Sadly, many continue to reject our witness just as they rejected Christ's. With increasing pace and intensity, our testimony is shunned and is becoming at odds with the law of our land. Worldwide, believers are being harassed, silenced, imprisoned, tortured and frequently killed.

But Jesus was faithful and true to his witness throughout his life, despite its difficulties and horrific end, because he knew he was not lying.

Christ's witness was founded on the reality of God's presence, his experience of God's kingdom and the assurance of his purpose. Consequently, that confidence was all he required to endure whatever form of rejection humankind might throw at him.

Do we likewise believe without doubt in what we have heard and experienced? And if so, are we now fulfilling our roles as God's faithful witnesses?

TAKE IT FURTHER

Reflect

We can all probably recognise parts of our lives in which we are not witnessing as faithfully as we would like. So let's renew our dependency on the Holy Spirit to reveal Christ to us through the word and our personal experience. The Spirit himself is a witness to and through us, enabling us to experience the kingdom, character and purpose of God, as he now indwells our lives (Acts 5:32).

Let's also consider the courtroom scenario referred to earlier. You are being observed and listened to by a jury—people with whom you come into contact through your daily routines, responsibilities and relationships.

What witness are you giving them concerning God's kingdom?

- Who or what would someone else perceive as your priorities in life, by what they see filling your time, attention and conversation?
- What motivates, drives or inspires you?
- If others had access to your bank account statements, what evidence would they see there concerning your use and handling of the resources that God provides to support you and others in furthering his kingdom work?

Take action: 'Seek first his kingdom and his righteousness, and all these things will be given to you as well' (Matthew 6:33).

What witness are you giving them concerning God himself?

There can sometimes be a temptation to create a god of our own imagination—to ask things of him that are contrary to his word and character, or expect him to change in line with our culture and social climate. We may even find ourselves seeking to live up to our own definition of 'righteous godly living' and, in turn, heap legalistic expectations on others to live by the letter of the law, rather than the spirit.

- Do you ever bear false witness in this way to who God truly is?
- What kind of characteristics do others see in you? Do your words and behaviour reflect God's character or do they simply blend in with the ways of a world that has no time for him?

Take action: 'Be imitators of God, therefore, as dearly loved children, and live a life of love, just as Christ loved us and gave himself up for us as a fragrant offering and sacrifice to God... Make every effort to live in peace with everyone and to be holy; without holiness no one will see the Lord... Live such good lives among the pagans that, though they accuse you of doing wrong, they may see your good deeds and glorify God on the day he visits us' (Ephesians 5:1–2; Hebrews 12:14; 1 Peter 2:12).

What witness are you giving them concerning God's purpose?

God desires for 'all people to be saved and to come to a knowledge of his truth' (1 Timothy 2:4). Is that purpose in evidence in your life? Given time, would others recognise that you're using your talents, resources and relationships in seeking to fulfil his purpose?

Take action: 'You are the light of the world. A city on a hill cannot be hidden. Neither do people light a lamp and put it under a bowl. Instead they put it on its stand, and it gives light to everyone in the house. In the same way, let your light shine before others, that they may see your good deeds and praise your Father in heaven' (Matthew 5:14–16).

Pray

Let us give thanks to God, 'who always leads us in triumphal procession in Christ and through us spreads everywhere the fragrance of the knowledge of him'. (2 Corinthians 2:14)

Read

Revelation 1:1–6; 3:14; John 8:12–59

JESUS:
THE GOOD SHEPHERD

'Save your people and bless your inheritance; be their shepherd and carry them for ever,' the psalmist cried (Psalm 28:9), and, while God promised to be the shepherd of his covenant people (Ezekiel 34:11–12), in time that prayer was answered in the person of Christ.

'I am the good shepherd,' Jesus declared (John 10:11), painting his self-portrait on a background of prophecy imbued with the dramatic strength of character, the rich colour of life and the intricate detail of intimacy suggested by this cherished term.

Listening to their master, the disciples didn't picture lush Cotswold hillsides, Western breeds of sheep, green wellies, sheepdogs or even farmers on quad-bikes rounding up their flocks (a sight I was bemused to watch quite recently). In fact, shepherds were such a routine sight as they walked the Judean uplands that the disciples required no further explanation to bring to mind the shepherd's traditional attire: a thick woollen cloak in which he would sleep or which he could fold into a padded seat, a staff (or wooden pole) in his hand, a rod hanging from his belt and a food bag containing dried fruit, olives, cheese or bread.

Moreover, the disciples lived in communities that were dependent upon sheep for wool, milk, sacrificial offerings and, occasionally, meat—a culture providing ample opportunity to understand and engage with shepherd temperaments. It's that personal familiarity that we may be lacking, living in the 21st-century West. While Renaissance portraits and Bible encyclopedias help us to imagine what they looked like, we also need to understand their character, which will help us to relate with our own good shepherd.

UNDERSTANDING THE IMAGE

First-century Palestinian shepherds were a hardy breed of men —weather-beaten, resilient to living and sleeping outdoors, strong enough to carry full-grown sheep and fit enough to trudge for miles across rough, stony plateaux and hills. They were brave, too, and thought nothing of fighting a gang of thieves, a jackal, fox, lion or bear, in order to save their sheep, often getting injured in the process and sometimes even losing their lives.

Nor were they unskilled. They could wield their rod—a cudgel or wooden club studded with nails at one end—in attack or defence, and they could handle a leather sling. In fact, their aim was so precise that, when need arose, they could land a stone right next to a sheep's nose to warn it against straying and encourage it back to the flock.

It was devotion to the sheep, however, that developed these strong and capable men—dedication that kept the sheep's best interests at heart. The constant companionship bonded shepherd with flock, and so they fondly called each sheep by name (names often relating to their colouring: Brown-foot or Black-tail, for example).

Gnarled but gentle hands tested for broken bones, removed thorns from faces and anointed cuts with oil. Observant eyes kept watch for predators, but also for the welfare of the sick, lame, pregnant and newborns.

Furthermore, each shepherd took responsibility for finding fresh pasture and gently flowing water—places providing rest, refreshment and nourishment. And so, he walked out in front, leading the sheep along his chosen route, calling to them to keep following, yet willing to abandon the flock to search for any that had strayed.

Such was his loving devotion to each individual that he would seek out the lost, disentangle brambles from a caught-up fleece or use his staff to haul up those that fell over ledges or into unseen pits. His calming presence would allay their fear as he carried them back to the others.

The shepherd's unceasing vigilance, patience, guidance, loyalty and sacrificial care provide an awesome portrait of Christ's love for his people. So let's consider how these historic shepherding facts can help us engage with our own good shepherd today.

JESUS, OUR SHEPHERD

David said, 'The Lord is my shepherd' (Psalm 23:1)—not 'our', 'your' or 'her', but 'my'. No matter whether we're new to the faith or long-term disciples, Jesus is intimately acquainted with us. He knows what happened yesterday and can see what lies ahead; and right now he is with us, watching over us with constant loving care. He knows the very number of hairs on our head and calls us each by name (Luke 12:7; John 10:3).

In the hurly-burly bustle of life or the isolation of housebound frailty; in the joys and sorrows, the ups and downs, the familiar and unexpected, the good shepherd longs to give us his best—life in abundant fullness (John 10:10).

But it's up to us to reach out and receive it. He won't force us to our knees, pin us to the ground or drag us along on a lead; rather, he waits for us to know and appreciate who he is, and thereby find the assurance we need to seek rest in the place of his presence.

- Are we willing to 'lie down in green pastures'? (Psalm 23:2a)? Are we resting in the place Christ has chosen for us, trusting him for provision, purpose, fulfilment and worth in life, or are we scurrying about as we try to provide such nourishment for ourselves? Life's seasons may change but the Lord's provision and care are constant. 'I am the gate; all who enter through me will be saved. They will come in and go out, and find pasture' (John 10:9).
- Are we willing to be led? Our good shepherd knows that his sheep must drink deeply to receive sufficient strength to cope with the heat of the day. And so, he seeks to restore our souls by leading us 'beside quiet waters' (Psalm 23:2b). Are we willing for him to lead us or do we prefer to follow our own inclinations, schedules or temporary titillations or the expectations of others? If the latter, we

can hardly grumble when energy, motivation or inspiration dips, when juggling our responsibilities leaves life feeling full but far from the inspired, passionate abundance promised by Christ.

- Are we straying from his presence? There are predators and pitfalls on our journey too, in the guise of cultural unbelief, materialistic pressures, immoral influences, the preoccupations of busyness and unseen spiritual forces of evil, to name just a few. The good shepherd is ready with rod to oust these predators, but only while we stay close. He'll zip a warning our way when we're straying too far from his presence—but, again, it's our choice to respond. If we ignore his convictions to our conscience, he cannot be blamed when we fall into the snares that stifle the breath from our spiritual life. That said, he will always come looking for us and offer his help to take us back to safety, if we want it and are willing to do it his way.

- Do we trust him for the unknown? Not every difficult situation implies that we have strayed from his protective presence. The very nature of the shepherd is to lead his sheep along the right path rather than the wrong one. The 'paths of righteousness' in Psalm 23:3b do not in themselves make us 'righteous', but they are the 'right' paths for us, in keeping with the good shepherd's foreknowledge, purpose and desired destination. Right paths take us through green pastures, but also through ominous valleys. Adversity, and even walking in the shadow of death, need cause us no fear while we keep following Jesus. Do we trust him with the insecurity of the unknown?

- Are we listening for the comfort of his familiar guiding voice? The shepherds of Israel are known for their unique calls—warbling cries, tones and intonations that, no matter how cleverly mimicked, were never confused by a shepherd's own flock, the sheep who had grown to know him. So let's take time to know our shepherd, too, as we listen in prayer, learn through the word and keep in step with the ways of the Holy Spirit—ever engaging with the voice and presence of the good and faithful shepherd of our souls.

TAKE IT FURTHER

Reflect

God may be challenging us to step out in faith with a new job, ministry or situation. He may be disciplining aspects of our lifestyle or behaviour, permitting difficult circumstances or encouraging us through a season of abundant spiritual fruit. But no matter how we perceive our present path, Jesus remains the good shepherd. Are we taking time to know and engage with this comforting, trustworthy character?

Pray

Good shepherd of my soul, thank you for the comfort, security, guidance and fulfilment promised to me as I follow your paths. In faith, I ask you to help me hear and recognise your voice above the many distractions and difficulties of life. Amen

Read

Psalm 23:1–4; Ezekiel 34:1–16; Luke 15:1–7; John 10:1–18

JESUS:

THE HEAD OF THE CHURCH

Have you ever been invited to tea with the Queen or to have dinner with the Prime Minister? Maybe you've attended a royal garden party or have been introduced to our most eminent politician at some auspicious occasion? Perhaps they have even come to your bedside, should you happen to have been in hospital during one of their official visits.

If we live in England, we recognise the Queen as the head of the country, albeit with many responsibilities legally delegated to 'her' government. Consequently, we also recognise the Prime Minister as the active head, implementing laws and directing the course of social welfare, healthcare, education, justice, finance and so on.

He (or she) is the head—the leader—and we are his (or her) people. A few of us may call ourselves acquaintances, friends or even family of our head, but the majority of us have limited communication, if any, with them. We live and work under their direction but without any meaningful relationship.

Such a scenario was never God's intention when he made Jesus 'the head of the church' (Ephesians 5:23). Although we are obliged to obey his commands and follow his direction, his role as head of the church is imbued with so much more than simply officiating as 'leader' of a company of believers. Rather, we who make up his church have become united to him—and therein lies a wonderful truth, the essence of what this role implies.

God placed all things under his feet and appointed him to be head over everything for the church, which is his body, the fullness of him who fills everything in every way. (Ephesians 1:22–23)

When we speak of 'the church', we might imply a religious establishment, an organisation or a building where believers meet. But when we consider Jesus as the head of the church, it is essential that we appreciate what it actually is. The church is not a lifeless institution or simply a group of adherents to a religious faith; it is a living organism. It is a body; moreover, it is Christ's own body. And we all know that a body cannot survive unless it remains connected to its life-giving head.

The head contains and protects the brain—that which sustains the effective working of vital body systems and coordinates all activities; the source of wisdom and knowledge, the centre of communication, perception and guidance.

Jesus is God's gift to the church. As head, he both leads and energises his body—individuals like you and me who obey his commands and, together, manifest him to the world as he delegates his divine authority and fills us with himself. He isn't just the CEO: he is the life-source flowing through the limbs and torso.

In first-century Israel, Jesus took on human flesh. He had his own body through which he could make God known to the world—his divine power, his God-given authority over evil, his obedient lifestyle to his Father's ways and will, his character and, of course, his love, which perfectly reflected God's love for humankind.

Today, we are his 'flesh and blood', and he wants to fill his body, the church, as he filled his own human body. Indeed, as Christ's church, we are supposed to be filled with all the fullness of God (Ephesians 3:19).

It is from our 'head' that we, his body, receive God's direction and are equipped with his capability, enabled to grow, resourced for his purposes and filled with abundant, eternal life. And, as each one of us is a part of his body, we depend on one another to receive Christ in full, enabling us to fulfil his purposes.

We cannot do it in isolation; nor can we do it in a limited 'holy huddle'. We need everyone because 'the body is not made up of one part but of many. If the foot should say, "Because I am not a hand, I do not belong to the body," it would not for that reason cease to be part of the body… If the whole body were an eye, where would the sense of hearing be? If the whole body were an ear, where would the sense of smell be? But in fact God has arranged the parts in the body, every one of them, just as he wanted them to be. If they were all one part, where would the body be? As it is, there are many parts, but one body. The eye cannot say to the hand, "I don't need you!" And the head cannot say to the feet, "I don't need you!"' (1 Corinthians 12:14–21).

It is only as we each do our part, especially chosen for us in advance by God (Ephesians 2:10), that Christ's body will function properly, energised and directed by the head.

Consequently, we must remain obedient to and dependent on Jesus, the head, as our source of life, power, direction, movement, perception, coordination, unity, health and, consequently, growth.

Is this our understanding of Jesus? Is this how we relate to the head of the church? Or do we just acknowledge him as our ruler—an impersonal authority whose ways and will we merely expect to be administered through 'church leaders'?

DON'T BE A HEADLESS CHICKEN!

Read Colossians 2:6–19. The familiar expression 'running around like a headless chicken' describes a very busy person doing lots of things but without doing anything effectively. It developed from the fact that it isn't unusual to see freshly decapitated chickens flopping around for a few moments, even running for a few seconds, wildly flapping their wings— this being the result of adrenalin in the muscle tissues giving the birds convulsions and the appearance of being alive.

In Colossians 2, Paul warns us not to be deceived and cut off from the reality of Christ by hollow philosophy, human traditions and mere adherence to religious observance (vv. 8, 16). He recognises individuals exhibiting false humility, whose minds are puffed up with idle notions concerning their perceived spirituality (v. 18), and writes that they have 'lost connection with the Head, from whom the whole body, supported and held together by its ligaments and sinews, grows as God causes it to grow' (v. 19).

In other words, it is possible to lose connection with our head, Jesus, and yet maintain the appearance of still being alive—of still being connected to our spiritual source of life. Our natural capabilities and endless hours of self-effort can, for a time, mask the reality that we are no longer being empowered by Jesus.

So let's consider the following questions.

Have I lost connection with the head?

- Am I 'running around like a headless chicken', wearing myself out to get everything done but without doing anything effectively?
- Have I become sidetracked by 'idle notions' concerning my spiritual experiences?
- Have I been led astray or am I trying to worship and serve God by rules only taught by human beings?
- Jesus quoted Isaiah to his religious contemporaries, saying, 'These people honour me with their lips, but their hearts are far from me. They worship me in vain; their teachings are merely human rules' (Matthew 15:8–9; Isaiah 29:13). Is this how he would describe the body in which we play our part today?

Jesus wasn't concerned so much with our form of religion as with our human nature. He still longs to see us transformed and renewed as we maintain our connection with him.

As individuals, each with a role to play as part of his body, we are all accountable to maintaining our own connection to the head so that his body—the church—will continue to be infused with the power, character and purpose of God.

So then, just as you received Christ Jesus as Lord, continue to live in him, rooted and built up in him, strengthened in the faith as you were taught, and overflowing with thankfulness… For in Christ all the fullness of the Deity lives in bodily form, and you have been given fullness in Christ, who is the head over every power and authority. (Colossians 2:6–7, 9–10)

Am I motivated by love?

Speaking the truth in love, we will in all things grow up into him who is the Head, that is, Christ. From him the whole body, joined and held together by every supporting ligament, grows and builds itself up in love, as each part does its work. (Ephesians 4:15–16)

Growth, as well as every other activity, depends on a healthy connection to our life-source. The body—the church—is utterly dependent on Jesus for growth. Each part of the body needs to grow in harmony with itself, in order to grow in a healthy way.

- Do I recognise that I am part of this 'living organism' or am I isolating myself, trying to 'grow' on my own?
- Am I more concerned about my own individual needs and preferences for spiritual growth or am I concerned for the whole—for the growth of each member and consequently the whole body?

Indeed, if we seek the good of everyone else through loving words and actions, the resultant environment is sure to attract numerical growth as well. 'Now you are the body of Christ, and each one of you is a part of it' (1 Corinthians 12:27).

JESUS:
THE HOLY ONE

'Holy' isn't an easy word to define: after all, it points to the infinite essence of the Almighty that shall forever remain incomprehensible to mere mortals. In fact, the name 'Holy One' reminds us that God is wholly different from human beings: 'I am God, and not a human being—the Holy One among you' (Hosea 11:9).

Nevertheless, scripture urges us 'mere mortals' to seek to be holy ourselves. If we undervalue the importance of that instruction, we may give the Holy One a bad press among unbelievers, including those who understandably use the derogatory term 'holier-than-thou' to describe an offensive display of pious self-righteousness.

Since time began, men and women have revered God's holiness. 'Who among the gods is like you, O Lord? Who is like you, majestic in holiness? … He is a holy God… Exalt the Lord our God… for the Lord our God is holy… Holy, holy, holy is the Lord Almighty' (Exodus 15:11; Joshua 24:19; Psalm 99:9; Isaiah 6:3).

Only in Jesus, however, who shares his Father's title, was the Holy One revealed in personal relationship with imperfect, unholy people. The angel announced it (Luke 1:35), demons acknowledged it (Mark 1:24), Peter proclaimed it (John 6:69; Acts 3:14) and the name shall apply to him for ever (Revelation 16:5).

But 'Holy One' isn't merely a title or description to acknowledge from a distance. It is because Christ is the Holy One that he in turn can make us holy.

CHRIST MAKES US HOLY

While my daughter was training to be a vet, she was on a particular farm placement where an orphaned newborn lamb was introduced to another ewe-mother whose own lamb had died. The ewe sniffed at the little lamb but, recognising that it wasn't hers, wouldn't have anything to do with it, shunning it from her presence and her vital supply of life-giving milk.

However, the farmer didn't give up and clothed the lamb in the bloody fleece of the ewe's own lamb which had died. Once again he introduced them to each other: this time the ewe took a sniff and welcomed the newborn to her udder.

'I am the Lord, who makes you holy' (Exodus 31:13). By God's will 'we have been made holy through the sacrifice of the body of Jesus Christ once for all' (Hebrews 10:10). Unless we are clothed in the holiness of Christ's perfect blood, we cannot approach God's presence. Only Jesus, the Holy One, can make us holy so that we can be reconciled to God and receive our source of eternal, spiritual life.

I trust that most, if not all, who are reading this have accepted Christ as Lord and received his free gift of salvation, which clothes us with his holiness. But if you haven't made that step of faith, then please don't delay. Just as that cute but needy lamb had to be 'clothed' with the ewe's own offspring before she would accept it, no matter how needy or seemingly 'good' we are, we must be clothed in Christ's holiness before God can receive us as his own.

CALLED TO BE HOLY...

As always, the names and descriptions of Jesus call for a response in believers, too, as we continue the process of working out our salvation (Philippians 2:12).

Paul addressed his first letter to the Corinthian church 'to those sanctified in Christ Jesus and called to be holy' (1 Corinthians 1:2). He recognised that believers are already sanctified—that is, made holy—through their faith in Christ's atoning death, but reminded them that they (and we) are still 'called' to live holy lives.

It's an active choice rather than a passive assumption, to respond to the ways of the Holy Spirit, who constantly works to transform us into the likeness of Christ (2 Corinthians 3:18). Knowing we are saved can tempt us to excuse or justify unholy traits in our attitudes or behaviour, but a number of reasons, including the following, should motivate us otherwise.

To fulfil our purpose

In our dining room, we have a number of electric sockets that can be used to plug in any electrical appliance. There is one, however, that has been wired in such a way that it can only be used for a lamp: it is set apart for that sole purpose.

Similarly, we were once free to live our lives as we wanted, but now we have been set apart—called to be holy in all we say and do.

It's not unusual to hear of Christians asking God to reveal his purpose for their lives, but, whether or not we currently think we've identified our divinely appointed role, one thing is for certain: we have all been given the purpose of living holy lives. This calling was bestowed on us as soon as we accepted the Holy One, Jesus, as Lord.

Do you not know that your body is a temple of the Holy Spirit, who is in you, whom you have received from God? You are not your own; you were bought at a price. Therefore honour God with your body… As obedient children, do not conform to the evil desires you had when you lived in ignorance. But just as he who called you is holy, so be holy in all you do; for it is written: 'Be holy, because I am holy.' (1 Corinthians 6:19–20; 1 Peter 1:14–16)

Christ has effectively 'rewired' us: he has made us holy and has set us apart to live holy lives, which God may subsequently use as he determines. And it's when we recognise and accept our purpose to be holy, walking in step with the ways of the Holy Spirit as our primary concern each day, that God will then choose how he wants to work to fulfil his sovereign purpose through our dedicated lives.

To be useful to God

I have a selection of kitchen knives and implements, which I try to keep sharp with my steel. I enjoy cooking but there's nothing more frustrating than reaching for a tool, only to find it blunted through lack of maintenance, chipped through misuse or even missing from the place where I expect it to be. Maybe God feels frustration at times when he reaches out to use my life, only to find that he first has to clean, oil, sharpen or mend where I've neglected its holy upkeep! Perhaps there are times when I've walked so far from his holy ways that I'm not even in the place he expects to find me—physically, mentally, emotionally or spiritually.

Indeed, the Holy One has made us holy in order to make us useful to God's purposes, not the other way around. 'In a large house there are articles not only of gold and silver, but also of wood and clay; some are for noble purposes and some for ignoble. Any who cleanse themselves from the latter will be instruments for noble purposes, made holy, useful to the Master and prepared to do any good work' (2 Timothy 2:20–21).

Our motive in seeking to please God through living holy lives is not to earn his favour but to provide him with useful tools. When we're prepared and at hand, he will use us and, in turn, reveal himself to others through our dedicated, holy lives.

To reveal God to others

'Huh—call yourself a Christian?!' If that's never been said to us personally, then most of us will know that it has been said of someone else who seems to be behaving contrary to the holy ways of God.

So we are reminded that we must 'make every effort to live in peace with everyone and to be holy; without holiness no one will see the Lord' (Hebrews 12:14). We'll never be perfect but we do have an obligation to seek to reflect Christ's holiness if we profess to follow him.

God has revealed himself to his people through creation, supernatural intervention and prophetic messages, but his ultimate strategy is to reveal himself to the world through the channel of surrendered, holy lives. Consequently, Peter instructs us to 'live such good lives among the pagans that, though they accuse you of doing wrong, they may see your good deeds and glorify God on the day he visits us' (1 Peter 2:12).

To please God

Finally, in all these things we seek to be holy in order to please the Holy One. Although we can never earn his sanctification, love, blessings or favour, the way that we live our lives can either please him or grieve him. If we truly love and appreciate him, we surely won't want to sadden his Spirit through unholy behaviour (Ephesians 4:29–31); rather, let us live to bring him pleasure.

TAKE IT FURTHER

Reflect

'The holy God is distinguished by righteousness' (Isaiah 5:16, HCSB). What distinguishes you?

Pray

Lord, here I am, set apart to bring you adoring worship and to offer you a holy temple through which you may influence others.

Read

You may like to take time to read and reflect upon the various scripture references mentioned in the study above, but also take a look at Leviticus 11:44–45.

JESUS:
OUR HOPE

If I could ask, 'What are you currently hoping for?' I guess that all your responses would be many and varied in both content and significance. Perhaps just a few might read something like these.

- I'm feeling increasingly frustrated in my current employment and hope that my recent application to another situation will prove successful.
- My husband and I have been trying for a baby for over two years without success; I'm hoping this month will prove to be different.
- There's a threat of redundancy at work at the moment but I can't afford to lose my job as I won't be able to keep up the mortgage payments. I really hope the company keeps me on.
- My daughter has found a lump in her breast and is waiting for the results of some tests. I desperately hope this isn't what we think it might be.
- I've been asked to speak at a women's retreat and I hope the Lord will use me to encourage them.

- An elder at our church was recently involved in a terrible car accident and is currently on a life-support machine. We are praying for him and his family and hoping that God will heal him.
- I am embroiled in a legal dispute that has been running on for months and is wearing me into the ground. I hope it is resolved very quickly.
- My eldest is leaving for university soon and I'm worried he will succumb to unhelpful influences. I hope he joins the Christian Union to help keep him on track.
- I've been invited to a big birthday party next week and am hoping to find an affordable outfit that I'll feel good in for the occasion.
- We're going away on holiday at the weekend and we hope it's going to be sunny.

We all hope for things for ourselves and others, and even for people we may not know but for whom we are touched with compassion. But whether our hopes are based on life-threatening circumstances or fanciful daydreams, they lack certainty; and so, depending on how important they are, our sense of self-worth, security or emotional well-being may be crushed if those hopes don't materialise. Consequently, they can affect the way we feel about ourselves, our loved ones, our world and even our faith if they take so much of our time and attention that they distract us from our overriding eternal hope encompassed in Jesus.

That said, it may not be easy to appreciate the relevance of our eternal hope when present circumstances are so distressing, confusing or just dull and mundane that they dominate our thoughts and emotions. So let's remind ourselves what Jesus 'our hope' implies for the future and how we can make that relevant to everyday life right now.

THE CERTAINTY OF OUR HOPE

In English, we use the word 'hope' while we wait to see whether a particular desire will actually be fulfilled. There may be good reasons to feel confident that it will happen, but there always remains an element of uncertainty until, one way or another, that hope is satisfied or dashed.

In the Bible, however, 'hope' is translated from a Greek word conveying absolute certainty. We don't say, 'I've accepted Jesus as my Lord and Saviour so I hope I will go to heaven'; rather, with absolute assurance we can say, 'I *am* going to heaven!' And so we praise God, for 'in his great mercy he has given us new birth into a living hope through the resurrection of Jesus Christ from the dead, and into an inheritance that can never perish, spoil or fade—kept in heaven' (1 Peter 1:3–4).

Fantastic! No matter how many more days or years we have on this earth, and whatever joys or trials we'll encounter, we have no doubt that eternal life and a heavenly inheritance await us—a divine birthright so immensely glorious as to encourage us to persevere through the life we live today.

But does it? Or does our hope for eternal life feel so far out of reach that the reality of 'today' overwhelms, discourages, frightens or deflates us?

THE SECURITY OF OUR HOPE

Storms will inevitably batter our lives. We aren't protected from experiencing trouble or hardship simply because we are Christian believers: we shall inevitably suffer dashed hopes to one degree or another. But in Jesus—our only assured hope—we can know peace.

The book of Hebrews tells us, 'We have this hope as an anchor for the soul, firm and secure' (6:19). Just as an anchor secures a ship in a position of safety, so Jesus, our hope, moors us to God. He is the only one who will not let us go and in whose promises we have absolute confidence (v. 18).

No matter how battered or bruised we may feel by the storm, if we hold on to our hope, Christ's peace will dispel our fears. For this 'living hope' isn't restricted to a spiritual eternity, but is alive for us today, offering an anchor for the whole of life. It is 'firm and secure': it cannot be moved by outside influences, provided we put our trust in its mooring.

And that, perhaps, is the big question facing some of us. Do we really trust in the purpose of the anchor and the trustworthiness of the one to whom it is moored? After all, ship anchors do occasionally fail, tearing loose of their mooring in terrific seas or succumbing to the inevitable rusting over many years, which is bound to weaken their intrinsic strength.

Not so with God. Our hope—our anchor, Jesus—'enters the inner sanctuary behind the curtain' (Hebrews 6:19). This is an image of the earthly tabernacle, pertinent to early church readers but pointing towards the sanctuary in heaven and the very presence of God, 'where moth and rust do not destroy' (Matthew 6:20) and destructive storms are eternally stilled (Revelation 21:4).

It is that assured hope for the future, to which we are moored, that enables us to persevere, despite the storms and insecurities of today.

THE ASSURANCE OF OUR HOPE

Writing this article has come at an apt time. Only last night, I was left alone in an unfamiliar place, my stomach churning with anxiety as I considered certain events unfolding around me. Desperate prayers that 'my hopes' would be fulfilled failed to restore inner calm, until a picture formed in my mind's eye—that of a tear-stained little girl with her tiny fists clenched shut against the open hand of her father. Gently, lovingly, he encouraged her to let go of what she was holding, as it really belonged to him, asking her to trust him to do what he knew best with it.

And so she did. I did. A little reluctantly at first, perhaps, but that gesture of faith, of unclenching my fists, letting go of the way I wanted my hope to be fulfilled and trusting my Father with its outcome, subsequently flooded my heart with his peace and assurance. It turned my focus away from my personal wish, back on to my assured hope, and helped me to view life from God's eternal perspective and purpose rather than from my own blinkered viewpoint.

It's not wrong to have wishful hopes and dreams, but they do need to be accompanied with the attitude of Christ, who always sought his Father's glory. In so doing, he was able to express his Gethsemane desire to be freed of imminent torture and yet sincerely follow up his appeal with, 'yet not my will, but yours be done' (Luke 22:42). In other words, 'Although I would hope that such-and-such would happen, I trust the outcome into your hands and that, in so doing, you will keep me in your perfect will.'

THE FOCUS OF OUR HOPE

Today, I'm aware of an incredible transformation in my attitude regarding my situation. Where just a few hours ago I felt resentful that God might not fulfil what I was hoping for, now, as I have genuinely sought God's glory in my life and actively placed my focus on my eternal hope, renewing my trust in his promises, his Spirit within has transformed my wish into the vision and purpose he has for my life.

So whether it's the gut-wrenching disappointment of dashed hopes or the immense relief and excitement of hopes fulfilled, let's seek today to place our wants in the light of Jesus. For if we focus first on our hope in him—his promises for the present and the future, and our need to accept and surrender to his ways—our hearts will naturally open to his presence, allowing him to flood them with his all-surpassing peace as he dovetails our hopes into his eternal perspective.

TAKE IT FURTHER

Reflect

The way we answer the questions, 'Do I truly want to glorify God through my life?' and 'Do I really trust in God's promises?' will reveal whether or not we really know Jesus as our hope—not just in theory, not just for the future, but in the practical outworking of life today.

Pray

Lord, I pray that you will be glorified in my life as I learn to trust my hopes in your promise that you will never leave me or forsake me, and that you hold my days in your hands. Amen

Read

Hebrews 6:13–20; 1 Peter 1:13; 3:15; Titus 1:1–2

JESUS:
OUR HUSBAND

The analogy of God committing himself as a husband to his bride, Israel, is a regular theme throughout the Old Testament. Isaiah proclaimed, 'Your maker is your husband—the Lord Almighty is his name' (Isaiah 54:5), while, through his prophet Jeremiah, the deserted 'husband' cried out for his bride to come back: 'Return, faithless people, for I am your husband' (Jeremiah 3:14). Consequently, it comes as no surprise that Paul identified Jesus as the 'husband' of his people (2 Corinthians 11:2) who together are the Church—his bride (Revelation 19:7).

It certainly is a tender analogy. Intending to woo his people back to himself (Hosea 2:14–15), God again brought up the marriage theme through the message of Hosea, with its affectionate contrast of 'master' and 'husband': 'You will call me "my husband"; you will no longer call me "my master"' (v. 16).

Historically, the Israelites trembled at God's presence on Mount Sinai, offering obligatory obedience to his covenant commandments, lapsing into apathy and then deserting him for other gods and ungodly lifestyles. But God, the ever-faithful 'husband' of a faithless 'bride', tenderly called them to return, to renew their vows to the one who pledged to love them with an everlasting love and forgive their repentant hearts.

'I WILL BETROTH YOU TO ME FOR EVER' (HOSEA 2:19A)

My heart melts on reading this passage. It is a revelation of God's loving, demonstrative, caring, affectionate, yearning heart for his bride.

To 'betroth' in Israelite marriages meant more than a romantic proposal over a candlelit dinner for two; it involved parental negotiations and the settlement of a bride price, which the husband-to-be had to pay his prospective in-laws. After this, the bride was considered bound to the marriage covenant and belonging to her husband for life, even though some time would lapse before the full consummation of their relationship.

Rebekah's family accepted gold and silver jewellery, clothing and costly gifts from Isaac as her price (Genesis 24:50–53); Jacob offered Dinah to the man who had raped her for the price of circumcising every male in the city (Genesis 34) and David was asked to pay 100 Philistine foreskins for the hand of Saul's daughter Michal (1 Samuel 18:22–27).

But gold, clothing, camels or jewels (let alone foreskins) were a far cry from the bride-price God offered for his bride—a price including the attributes that he himself would bring into this intimate covenant relationship. God betroths his people to himself in righteousness, justice, love, compassion and faithfulness (Hosea 2:19b–20a); committing himself again to his beloved bride in his covenant role as sovereign and Lord.

He offers—indeed, promises—loyalty, honesty, uprightness and decency in all his dealings with her; equality and fairness in his relationships with his people, both in honouring his bride's obedience and correcting where correction is due; steadfast devotion and forgiveness; tender mercy, especially to those who are weak, needy, vulnerable or oppressed; and absolute dependability to all that he is and has promised he will do.

What a price—what a husband—perfectly revealed and paid for in Christ!

Yet the bride was obliged to play her part in the marriage covenant, too and, sadly, her faithlessness caused a separation. She heard her husband's warnings but preferred the adulterous life she had chosen—and, in time, found herself exiled from home. Our loving God is jealous for his bride and will do whatever he must to revive, re-ignite and restore her first love.

'AND YOU WILL ACKNOWLEDGE THE LORD' (HOSEA 2:20B)

God's bride is bound to commit herself to the terms of the covenant relationship as fully as her husband has committed himself to her. In Hosea's case, she sadly failed to do so, but the prophets foretold a future when separation would no longer be necessary, when the perfect sacrifice for the bride's rebellious sin would be offered once and for all.

Jesus lived the life that perfectly expressed the divine bride-price and died so that the price might be paid in full

(1 Corinthians 6:20). The covenant was renewed and now we await its full consummation. Meanwhile, however, the bride's husband is still jealous for our first love, for God never changes and 'the Lord, whose name is Jealous, is a jealous God' (Exodus 34:14).

It's funny how most people won't tolerate being two-timed and yet some reject our faith on the basis that God, after many warnings, allowed his adulterous, unrepentant bride to be disciplined in exile. They perceive the God of the Old Testament as harsh, forgetting the fact that his actions stemmed not from cruelty but from steadfast, uncompromising love.

God is a jealous husband because he loves his bride: after all, who isn't jealous for the love of the ones they love? And so, coming full circle, we find Paul deeply concerned for the Corinthian church, for whom he shares God's jealousy. 'I am jealous for you with a godly jealousy. I promised you to one husband, to Christ, so that I might present you as a pure virgin to him. But I am afraid that... your minds may somehow be led astray from your sincere and pure devotion to Christ' (2 Corinthians 11:2–3).

Indeed, the Corinthian church had been led astray by the teachings of false prophets (vv. 3–15). And here lies our challenge as we, 'the bride', commit to Christ 'our husband': are we upholding our side of the covenant or are we arousing his jealousy?

✳

ARE YOU A LOVING BRIDE?

We may feel that our personal prayers and worship are suffi-cient evidence that Jesus is our first love, but his jealousy may yet be aroused if that love is not proved in practice, for just as Christ loves us, so he expects us to love his people too.

So, let's take another look at our 'husband's' priceless bride-price (Hosea 2:19–20) and see whether we—his people, his bride—are upholding our part of the covenant or whether, like Corinth, our thoughts and our devotion to Christ have somehow been led astray.

Christ, our 'husband', offers his righteousness to cover our sinfulness, which reconciles us to God in loving relationship (Philippians 3:9).

- Are we still striving to be good enough for his love? Then let's accept our 'husband's' righteousness in faith and rest in the knowledge of our salvation.
- Are we fulfilling our side of the covenant by living not according to the sinful nature but according to the Spirit (Romans 8:3–7)?
- Are we imposing standards of our own making on other people before we love and accept them for who they are?
- Are we treating others in an upright and honourable manner?
- Have you 'put off your old self, which is being corrupted by its deceitful desires' and 'put on the new self, created to be like God in true righteousness and holiness' (Ephesians 4:22, 24)?

Christ, our 'husband', offers justice to all (Matthew 12:17–21).

- Are we treating all people equally or showing favour to certain individuals over others? (James 2:1)
- Are we more prone to encouraging others or rebuking them? Justice maintains the right balance. 'Encourage and rebuke with all authority. Do not let anyone despise you' (Titus 2:15).

Christ, our 'husband', loves us unconditionally. 'Greater love has no one than this, to lay down one's life for one's friends. You are my friends if you do what I command... This is my command: love each other' (John 15:13–14, 17).

- Are we loving God with all our heart, soul, mind and strength as Jesus commanded (Mark 12:30)?
- Do we truly love others as we love ourselves (v. 31) or are we freely receiving the love of God but only giving it out to those who we feel have earned or deserve it?
- Are we loving only according to how we feel or loving because we choose to?
- Does our declared love for Christ's people evidence itself in forgiveness (Matthew 6:14–15)?

Christ, our 'husband', is filled with compassion for his people and demonstrated his tender mercy to the hungry, the sick, the possessed, the lost and the outcast (for example, Mark 1:41).

- Do we merely pray for others or are we so mindful of their needs as to put our prayers into practice—offering our time, assistance, advice, care or provision? 'Whatever you did for one of the least of these brothers and sisters of mine, you did for me' (Matthew 25:40).

Christ, our 'husband', is faithful to all he has promised; he will never leave us or forsake us and promises to be with us always (Hebrews 13:5; Matthew 28:20).

- Do we respond to his commands with the dependability he deserves from us?
- Do we fulfil our God-given responsibilities using the talents and resources he has provided for that purpose? (Matthew 25:23)

This, then, is how we respond as the bride to the jealous love of our husband—loving him and so loving others with all that we are.

JESUS:
I AM

When I was a little girl, I gave each of my dolls and teddies carefully chosen names, solemnised in a little ceremony I'd devised to ensure they could never be changed: Ellie-Wellie, Monica, Cerenda (I couldn't pronounce 'Cinderella' at the time). Rowe, my very first fluffy companion, given to me when I was born, still has a place in my bedroom and bears her name with pride.

In my teens, I daydreamed about my own future children and what I might like to call them. That dream has never been realised, as my daughter was named before I adopted her, but friends of mine have shared their excitement, anguish and even disagreements over naming their own children—sometimes scouring the Bible or books for ideas, using a family name or praying for God to inspire them with one that might suit the person he created.

Names in biblical times, however, were even more significant than they are today. In fact, the names given to babies were often changed in adulthood to reflect the new role, position or character that a person had been given or acquired. Moses, for example, deliberately changed Hoshea to Joshua to reflect the new name of Israel's God on entering the promised land (Numbers 13:16); Nathan pronounced the name Jedidiah over Solomon, declaring God's favour on David's tenth son, which was later proved when, despite his sibling rank, he inherited his father's throne (2 Samuel 12:25); and Jesus renamed Simon as Peter, the disciple with the rock-like character whom Jesus could use to build his church (Matthew 16:17–18).

As names assigned to people were significant regarding their role or character, it follows that divine names carried tremendous implications, too. God had been known to the ancient patriarchs by various titles, such as El-Shaddai (God Almighty), El-Elyon (Most High God) and Adonai (Lord), for example. Other surrogate names can be found, too, like Jehovah Jireh (The Lord Will Provide). God never changed, but, as he revealed different aspects of himself to his people, they in turn summed up each new revelation in a new name or title, as a record for future generations of their deepening knowledge of God.

It was to Moses, however, that God gave the name he wanted to be known by, the name that would supersede all other names: Yahweh (Exodus 3:14–15; 6:2), meaning 'I Am Who I Am' (or 'I Will Be Who I Will Be'), often shortened to 'I Am'. ('Yahweh' may appear as a capitalised LORD in your Bible.)

This was the name God chose to express his character, dependability and faithfulness to his people—a title that urges a response of faith. Rather than limiting the revelation of his being to just one aspect, the seemingly obscure name 'I Am' expressed the infinite essence of God in all circumstances. God is as God does. He embodies the very meaning of the name that is subsequently revealed to, and experienced by, those who put their trust in that name.

In short, Yahweh—I Am Who I Am—is a dynamic name representing God's words and his actions; the initiative of how God will act and reveal himself remains with him, and is simply for us to discover.

Furthermore, this name was reserved for God alone, whose divine qualities could never be shared with mere mortals. Consequently, the command was given, 'You shall not misuse the name of the Lord [Yahweh] your God' (Exodus 20:7). So when Jesus faced his accusers and said, 'Before Abraham was born, I am!' it was immediately construed as blasphemy, and they picked up stones to stone him (John 8:58–59).

For those of us today who believe that Jesus is God's Son, this may seem like an overreaction. But in the eyes of his contemporaries and religious culture, he was simply a man— clever and capable, but just a man. Anyone who declared themselves equal with God by sharing the divine name committed blatant blasphemy.

In truth, however, Jesus was revealing to his generation the reason for which he had come—to make known the name of God. God's revelation in history had prepared the way for this unique revelation in Christ's birth, life, death and resurrection. In Jesus, the name of God—that is, his character, nature and purpose—were perfectly revealed.

Jesus often gave himself names that revealed specific manifestations of Yahweh's character, such as 'I am the good shepherd… the bread of life… the light of the world'. He also referred to Yahweh when he declared 'I am he' to the Samaritan woman at the well (John 4:25–26), to the fearful disciples as he walked on water (6:16–20) and to the guards who came to arrest him in Gethsemane (18:1–8).

In John 8:58 he simply, yet magnificently, declared, 'I am'. He didn't come into existence at a particular point in time; rather, his being is continuous. It always was, always is and always will be, for Jesus is God and, consequently, shares his name—his divinity and the initiative of how he chooses to make himself known.

His hearers knew about God, worshipped God and said that they knew him. In truth, 'I am' was standing right in front of them and they failed to recognise what their pre-conceptions and religious bias had blinded them to, so they picked up stones to stone him. On this occasion, however, Jesus slipped away to continue his mission of revealing the name of God through his person and actions. All that remained was to complete his mission of salvation.

And so, at the end of his earthly life, Jesus was able to pray, 'I have manifested your name to the people whom you gave me out of the world… I made known to them your name, and I will continue to make it known, that the love with which you have loved me may be in them, and I in them' (John 17:6, 26, ESV).

HOW DO YOU RESPOND TO 'I AM'?

In this book, we consider many names and titles that are given to Jesus in the Bible, but 'I Am' encompasses them all, and more. We may be inclined to come to Jesus as Protector, Shepherd, King and so on, but today we come to the one who effectively says, 'I am who I am, and will choose to be and do what I choose.'

Do we let Jesus be and do what he wants to be and do, or do we still try to give him a name (a type of character or purpose) that best fits what we want him to have and live up to? To help us answer, let's consider the following questions:

- Do we believe in Jesus as Comforter but falter in trusting him as Provider?
- Do we believe that he personifies Love but question him as the just Judge?
- Do we believe that he is implicit Truth but seek meaning and purpose from a life of our choosing, rather than the abundant life he has chosen and wants to give to us?
- Do we believe he is divine—he is God—or do our worries or our 'giving a helping hand' to situations reveal that we don't really believe in his overall authority as King?

In short, do we limit our worship, devotion and witness to the aspects and purposes of God that we are drawn to or prefer, or just hope that he might be?

When a young man was being harmed by an evil spirit, his father said to Jesus, 'If you can do anything, take pity on us and help us.'

'"If you can?" said Jesus. "Everything is possible for him who believes." Immediately the boy's father exclaimed, "I do believe; help me overcome my unbelief!"' (Mark 9:21–24).

We, too, may say we believe. But perhaps, from our response to the previous questions, we recognise that we also need help in our unbelief. Perhaps we have certain thought patterns or behaviour traits which betray the fact that our belief is limited to some elements of who Jesus is, lacking a full response of faith in 'I Am'.

If so, let's renew a personal response to the following scriptures.

Choose

'If serving [Yahweh] seems undesirable to you, then choose for yourselves this day whom you will serve.' (Joshua 24:15)

Will I choose to let Jesus be 'I am' and surrender to his will, his ways and his purposes? Or do I prefer to follow a god of my own imagining or the gods of success, materialism, prosperity, ease and many others that try to attract me?

Trust

Those who know your name will trust in you, for you, [Yahweh], have never forsaken those who seek you. (Psalm 9:10)

Do I truly know his name: Yahweh—I Am Who I Am? Do I know the one who embodies the very meaning of that name? Am I continuing to pursue and know Jesus with all my heart, mind, soul and strength, which in turn will deepen and strengthen my trust and faith in God?

Seek

My heart says of you, 'Seek his face!' Your face, [Yahweh], I will seek. (Psalm 27:8)

God made human beings in his own image, not the other way around. Let's determine to seek the right image of Yahweh in our prayers.

Let us acknowledge [Yahweh]; let us press on to acknowledge him. As surely as the sun rises, he will appear; he will come to us like the winter rains, like the spring rains that water the earth. (Hosea 6:3)

Read

Exodus 3:1–17; John 8:12–59

JESUS:
THE IMAGE OF THE INVISIBLE GOD

It was the sixth day of creation: light, sky, land, vegetation, sun, moon, stars, fish, birds and animals were all in place. But the new dawn heralded the supreme climax of divine handiwork—the creation of men and women. 'Then God said: "Let us make human beings in our image, in our likeness... So God created human beings in his own image, in the image of God he created them; male and female he created them"' (Genesis 1:26–27).

Destined for friendship with the divine, Adam and Eve enjoyed intimate acquaintance with God, walking and talking with him in the perfection of Eden. But one tragic day, they lost that privilege. They chose to do things their way rather than his and were banished from his holy presence. Sin did its utmost to mar the Creator's image in the created, and future generations would never see God face-to-face as Adam and Eve had done—at least, not this side of heaven.

Consequently, for thousands of years, God revealed himself to his beloved people through the beauty of his created world, supernatural power, divine intervention, messages to the prophets and the temple in Jerusalem.

But his revelation remained incomplete until he sent his

very own Son, Jesus. He who shared the nature of God from all eternity took on human flesh—first, that we may know and see God for ourselves; then, to restore to humanity the image and purpose we were intended to bear. 'The Son is the radiance of God's glory and the exact representation of his being' (Hebrews 1:3); 'He is the image of the invisible God' (Colossians 1:15).

At last, our picture is complete. By the indwelling of the Holy Spirit in his life and his perfect obedience to his Father's will, Christ revealed to his own generation and, through the Gospels, to all generations, the image of God whom no one has seen—the very essence of his nature, the perfect portrait of his character, the manifestation of his glory.

HIS BEAUTY

David yearned to gaze upon the breathtaking beauty of the Lord (Psalm 27:4). Indeed, there is no doubt that God is beautiful, as we see his splendour reflected in his creation.

The acts of humankind may have devastated rainforests, gouged hillsides with motorways, polluted oceans with scum, flattened countryside with concrete and filled skies with fumes, but the beauty of God's brushstrokes still bear their mark upon meadows of poppies, buttercups and daisies; the graceful willow and bright full moon; the sparkle of sunlight dancing on water; the brilliance of gardens cloaked in virgin snow; hedgerows adorned with dew-encrusted spider-silk; soaring eagles, vivid green woodpeckers, and palomino ponies cantering through fields.

As Jesus is the image of the beauty of God, we would expect him to share that beauty, but Isaiah foretold, 'He had no beauty or majesty to attract us to him, nothing in his appearance that we should desire him' (Isaiah 53:2). The brushstrokes of created beauty were inadequate cosmetics to groom his outward appearance, but his inward beauty was no less exquisite than the radiance of God's glory.

As rays of light pierce the darkness, so the glory of God, imbued in Christ, radiated from his being. He shattered the ugliness of sin as he mingled with his contemporaries. Such beauty is both perfect and permanent, unlike the fickle 'look' of today, the mask of make-up or even pretty flowers that so quickly fade away. The beauty of God does not wilt, wither or wrinkle: it is permanent and for ever, flowing from the eternal source of his holiness.

We may long to know we're beautiful in the eyes of the world as we squeeze our bodies into the latest fashions, hone our features with rouge, exercise, diet or even submit to the surgeon's knife so that we might look like our favourite models. I'm not condemning the way we choose to take care of our appearance or our physical health, but true beauty that restores the image of God in our lives does not come from outward appearance: it emanates from within. It springs from the holiness of God's Spirit indwelling our hearts and, as we keep in step with the ways of the Holy Spirit, so the beauty of God will radiate from our lives, infusing our speech and behaviour.

HIS MAJESTY

The Creator of the world is all-powerful, all-knowing, ruler of his world—and such grandeur and authority were, in part, displayed through his glorious temple residence in Jerusalem. God is omnipresent but he chose for himself a dwelling-place on earth where people might draw closer to him.

Palaces are homes for kings and queens; the temple was the home for God's Spirit, residing in the Most Holy Place between two golden cherubim. Not that his Spirit was accessible to the hoards of priests and pilgrims who worshipped in its courts, for only the high priest, once a year, was granted entrance to that innermost sanctuary. But the temple was built in accordance with God's own detailed plans—architecture, furnishings, décor and ministry that exalted his majestic authority; marble, gold, silver, gemstones, pillars, cloisters, courts and gateways, worthy of its sovereign resident.

'He had no beauty or majesty.' Jesus wasn't born in a palace; he didn't wear royal robes or eat using golden utensils. But he was the perfect temple of God's Holy Spirit—the first man born in whom God was pleased to permanently dwell.

Jesus was gentle and humble (Matthew 11:29), but that doesn't imply weakness. Rather, he was perceived as a man of authority (7:29). He didn't bow down to human expectations (Mark 1:35–38) and was determined to fulfil God's purposes, no matter what obstacles others placed in his way (Matthew 16:21–23; Luke 9:51–53).

Jesus placed children on his knee, touched the untouchables and wept in public, unashamed. But his divine authority overruled demonic forces (Mark 1:23–26; 5:1–13), his supreme wisdom confounded the teachers (Luke 2:41–47; Matthew 13:54), his powers amazed the disciples (Matthew 8:23–27), and his kingly countenance bewildered his guards (John 18:3–6).

And so, through his life, death and resurrection, the true majesty of King Jesus restored our God-given authority (Luke 10:19), divine counsel (John 14:26), supernatural power (14:12) and royal bearing (1 Peter 2:9). But with privilege comes responsibility: are we, like Jesus, willing to obey our Father, that we may experience the full measure of these promises?

HIS CHARACTER AND NATURE

I wonder how many descriptive words we might find in scripture that define God's character. Off the top of my head come faithful, loving, just, merciful, gracious, righteous, forgiving, compassionate, good… but there are so many more.

The prophets spoke about these attributes of the divine— words and, at times, bizarre yet symbolic behaviour that conveyed the essence of God as best they could to the people. But as helpful as their witness was, it was never complete until Jesus—who is God—fulfilled every facet in and through his perfect life.

We cannot overestimate the impact of his person. His whole life drew people towards him. Some chose to reject his claims, but all were amazed by his teaching, behaviour, miraculous powers—in fact, his very being.

No one has ever, or will ever, portray such an authentic representation of God, for there is only one Christ and he now sits at the right hand of his Father in heaven.

Nevertheless, Peter reminds us that we participate in the divine nature (2 Peter 1:3–4). The one who dwells within us by his Holy Spirit wants to express his perfect character through the vehicle of our lives. But are we willing to let him, as we submit to his ways? Do his grace, unconditional love and acceptance, forgiveness, justice and so on manifest themselves through us, or do our own responses get in the way?

The New Testament writers encourage us to 'flee' immorality, idolatry, the love of money and ungodly behaviour (1 Corinthians 6:18; 10:14; 1 Timothy 6:10–11); not to 'gratify the desires of the sinful nature', desires that result in acts of impurity, hatred, discord, jealousy, selfish ambition, envy, drunkenness and so on (Galatians 5:16); to 'put to death' whatever belongs to our earthly nature, be that lust, evil desires or greed (Colossians 3:5). All these instructions require an active response, that we might further express the qualities of God's nature. As we choose to let him have his way, our divine family likeness will begin to appear and so attract others to his glory.

Jesus came that we might see God. He died that we might know God. His resurrected life has opened the way for God's image to be known through our own lives by the power of his Holy Spirit, who is resident in our hearts. For 'we, who with unveiled faces all reflect the Lord's glory, are being transformed into his likeness with ever-increasing glory, which comes from the Lord, who is the Spirit' (2 Corinthians 3:18). All that remains is that we follow in his footsteps and seek to obey God's will.

TAKE IT FURTHER

Reflect

What do you find attractive about Jesus when you read about him in the Gospels? How might this encourage you to enable that family likeness to develop in your life?

Pray

Lord Jesus, we read in the Gospels that people were amazed when they spoke to you, watched you and received your love and healing. Lord, may your nature be reproduced in me, with ever-increasing measure.

Read

Hebrews 1:1–4; Colossians 1:15–23; 2 Peter 1:3–11

JESUS:
THE KING OF KINGS

One of many fond memories I have each Christmas recalls my senior-school carol service where, every year, the choir sang the Hallelujah Chorus from Handel's oratorio *Messiah*: 'King of Kings, for ever and ever, and Lord of Lords, Hallelujah! Hallelujah!'

I wasn't even a Christian when I first heard this fabulous piece of music, but that didn't stop me from joining the altos and belting out my own 'Hallelujah' to this King of kings with tremendous gusto.

Every year I find myself humming the tune as the Christmas season stamps its authority on the TV screen and the volumes of incoming post: images of a baby in a feeding trough, a bright shining star above a stable, Mary, Joseph, shepherds, magi, innkeepers, plus (of course) the gifts, decorated trees, cartoon characters, cute animals and doves, all vying for a place on our Christmas cards.

But, I wonder, who or what is vying for the attention of our hearts?

Christians naturally feel concerned that the secular consumerism surrounding Christmas today overshadows its true significance. We might discuss it (or even grumble about it) after Sunday services; we might pray about it; we may even feel the need to write to councillors who've attempted to scrap the word 'Christmas' from the high street for fear of causing offence. And all of these activities are good and necessary in their own way (except, perhaps, any fruitless grumbling).

Nevertheless, our greatest influence on today's 'winterval' festivities may actually come from our own response to the King of kings and our personal obligation to uphold his rightful place in the way we choose to celebrate. Perhaps, as we make that our chief concern, Christ will continue to attract worship from other people who subsequently meet him through us.

So, let's recall how the title 'King of kings' came about.

Of the increase of his government and peace there will be no end. He will reign on David's throne and over his kingdom... for ever. (Isaiah 9:7)

God is king over all the earth (Psalm 47:2, 6–9). Having first revealed and established his kingship in Israel, he passed its administration to Jesus so that, through his perfect sacrifice, all peoples of every nation might worship him as supreme King and be welcomed into God's kingdom (Daniel 7:13–14).

In fulfilment of prophecy, Jesus was born king of the Jews (Matthew 2:2). His genealogy highlights his royal ancestry, conferring on him his royal status, while his virgin birth verifies God as his Father.

His life's witness attested to his kingly powers over

human and spiritual authorities. His teaching centred on the kingdom of God and, at his trial, he admitted he was a king. Through his perfect sacrifice and resurrection, God exalted him to the place where every knee will bow at his name and, at the end of time, the King of kings will overcome all who rebel against him.

But it's not just a title for the historic past or heavenly future. It's a role that Christ continues to fulfil today.

On his robe and on his thigh he has this name written: KING OF KINGS AND LORD OF LORDS. (Revelation 19:16)

God, in his divine wisdom, has given authority to hundreds of men and women throughout the centuries to rule as kings or queens over different areas or peoples of the world. But overruling all these worldly kingdoms is the eternal kingdom of God, over which he has designated Christ as King—King of God's kingdom and, consequently, King of all the kings, imbued with divine power and authority.

It's a truth that can be difficult to comprehend as we continue to observe the ongoing atrocities that certain 'kings' inflict upon their subjects and neighbours in pursuit of power or to satisfy their greed. One might ask, if Christ is King of kings, why doesn't he overrule or dethrone them?

Although Christ the King holds the keys to the door of God's kingdom (Revelation 3:7–8), he has never established it by force. In fact, neither Herod nor Pilate understood the implications of Jesus' kingship. Herod tried to protect his own 'kingly power' by slaughtering the potential competition from among the little boys in and around Bethlehem

(Matthew 2:2–3, 16) and Pilate had Christ crucified in fear that this 'king of the Jews' might lead a rebellious uprising against the Roman occupation (John 18:33—19:1, 12–19).

All that these men knew of kingdoms was conquest by war, political scheming and domination through bribery or brutality—not so different from certain 'kingly authorities' today, who still try to suppress Christianity by force.

In contrast to the fleeting kingships of the world, however, Christ—the King whose primary command is love—offers to be king of our hearts for ever, and each of us must choose how we respond. Enjoying his love for us, loving God in return and expressing that love in practice to others is the fundamental essence of his kingdom.

'Where is the one who has been born king of the Jews? We saw his star in the east and have come to worship him.' (Matthew 2:2)

It's one thing to feel frustrated by the degeneration of Christmas celebrations into an excuse to spend, eat and drink too much, but we all have an obligation to follow the way of our King. Rather than trying to establish God's kingdom by force—through antagonistic debate, ungodly grumbling or critical attitudes, for example—let's seek to establish his kingdom through worshipping the King of kings. Worship isn't simply the passive expression of what we believe through song and prayer, while we hide behind the walls of a church building. True worship actively expresses itself through loving devotion and genuine surrender, manifest in our daily life, including our Christmas celebrations. In fact, that is the crux of the kingdom of God. It's the place where Christ the King is given full reign and authority, and that place is not a matter of geography but a matter of our hearts. Is Christ the true King of your heart or is someone or something else vying for your loyal attention?

HOW TO WORSHIP THE KING OF KINGS

Be honest

- Are we, like Herod, afraid of losing 'control' over our lives—fearful that submitting to Christ will erode our reputation, invite his authority over the things that we hold valuable, or knock us off the throne of the little kingdom of life that we cherish as 'ours'?
- Are we like the shepherds—interested, enquiring, seeking to find out what Christ's birth is all about, but, once it's all over, simply returning to our usual routines to get on with life as we did before?
- Are we like the magi, understanding a little without fully comprehending the whole of God's sovereign purpose, and yet eager to find and worship the King? If so, let's offer him our 'gold, frankincense and myrrh' as part of that act of worship: all our resources, whether of time, talent or money; all of our hearts, from where comes the sweet fragrance of loving adoration; and all that we are—the willing sacrifice of what we want from life, in order to fulfil what the King wants from our lives.

Only you and I can know what that loving response of worship will look like in practice, but the King of kings is surely a most worthy recipient.

Be alert

- We may call Jesus our King, but to what extent do the busy preparations for the festive season and the stress of meeting the 25 December deadline, on top of our usual obligations, distract us from worshipping him? Is there anything we need to change or reprioritise?
- Do we suffer a gnawing anxiety concerning the potential drain on limited finances, which, in turn, overshadows our trust in the King and the promised contentment found in pursuing his priorities? If so, do we need to cut down on our accustomed spending?
- Does the seasonal encouragement to meet with family and friends intensify in us feelings of loneliness, grief or hopelessness, shifting our focus from the joy of God's kingdom to the sad repercussions of a fallen world? If so, do we feel able to invite others into our home to host some celebrations ourselves?
- Are our hearts open to reach out to others who may live with such concerns?

Be open

- Inviting our unsaved family and friends to our church carol service is just one way in which we can introduce them to the King of kings.

- Our lifestyle and attitudes will also attract them if we genuinely exhibit the joy of God's kingdom of love, and can offer peace and purpose where others might be stressed, anxious or forlorn.
- During the weeks leading up to Christmas, how could our routine, contacts, preparations and invitations make a difference to someone's preconceived ideas about Christianity, Christmas and, ultimately, the King of kings?
- To what extent are we available to the King to enable him to make himself known to the 'shepherds, innkeepers, magi, Herods and Roman officials' of our day?

Pray

King Jesus, thank you for your willingness to leave the glories of heaven and live a life of human impoverishment, so that I may now enter your kingdom. I offer afresh all that I am, to allow you to share your kingdom of love with whomever you bring into contact with me, so that you may inspire an eager longing in their hearts to know and love you, too.

Read

Daniel 2:44–45; Revelation 17:14; 19:11–16

JESUS:
THE LAMB OF GOD

Imagine walking through your locality, to be confronted by someone pointing at a man and saying, 'Look, the Lamb of God, who takes away the sin of the world!' People without any experience of church would be forgiven for wondering where the cute, fluffy white animal was hiding. But even as Christians, while we may recognise the scene as coming from the New Testament, it's not always easy to explain its implications to an unbelieving generation, one that may even dismiss the practice of sacrifice as barbaric appeasement of brutal or imaginary gods.

So what exactly did John the Baptist mean when he spoke those words? And how can we explain this fundamental Easter message to our friends and family who've dismissed it as historic fable?

WHY THE ANALOGY OF A LAMB?

Aside from the obvious provision of meat, lambs played an essential part in Israel's history and religious life. When the people prepared to escape from Egyptian slavery, it was the blood of lambs without defect, painted on their door frames, that protected them from the angel of death. When the angel saw the blood, it passed over their homes without inflicting the plague on the firstborn (Exodus 11—12).

Furthermore, lambs without defect were used in a number of Levitical sacrifices. A person seeking God's forgiveness, for example, could do so by offering the blood of unblemished lambs on the altar of burnt offering (Leviticus 4:32–35). It was to such people, familiar with the atoning blood of lambs, that John made his pronouncement, at a time when temple sacrifice was at the heart of religious life.

'Look, the Lamb of God, who takes away the sin of the world' (John 1:29). John's analogy struck their hearts with its simple but profound truth—that here was a man who would provide a means to receive God's forgiveness; and not just for them, but for the whole world.

The impact on his hearers was immense, even life-changing (vv. 35–37), but today's generation may well retort, 'If God was really good and loving, why couldn't he forgive us without the need for sacrifice?' So we need to take this one step further.

WHY THE NEED FOR ANIMAL SACRIFICE?

When God created humankind, he gave them the fruit of the tree of life, by which they would live for ever. But when Adam and Eve chose to disobey God (which is the essence of sin), they were banished from the garden of Eden in which the tree of life grew, thereby succumbing to the consequence of their sin, which is death.

However, God didn't banish them to punish them. He did it to protect them. His immense holiness is far beyond anything we can truly understand with our finite minds. It is like a fire that consumes sin. To put it another way, because of his immense love for us, God will not remain in the presence of our sin (no matter how small or great we perceive our disobedience to be) for he knows that we could not survive his closeness (see Exodus 33:20; Isaiah 6:5).

Nevertheless, we were not left in exile from his presence. God introduced the means by which our sin could be removed from his sight, thereby restoring that broken fellowship—and this he did through sacrifice.

God is perfect in every way, and that includes being perfectly just, as well as forgiving. For God to forgive sin without justice being done—that is, without the consequences of sin being met (death)—would be a contradiction of his character. Consequently, it was out of love (not brutality) that God provided the means for the penalty of sin to be met by another living being—a principle introduced using animals, including lambs, offered in accordance with his holy code of law.

As a result of sacrifice, God was able to dwell among his people in the Most Holy Place of the tabernacle and, later, the Jerusalem temple. Pilgrims would come to the priest, offer their sacrifices to him, and, in so doing, be made acceptable to worship God in his house.

But, as satisfactory as that was externally, to make them ceremonially clean, the blood of animals could never provide the inward cleansing from sin that true intimacy with God requires. In fact, only the high priest, once a year, was permitted access to God's presence, to sprinkle the blood of sacrifice on behalf of the people's unintentional sins; and even that sacrifice was imperfect, as it had to be repeated year after year.

So animal sacrifice was merely preparing the way for the perfect sacrifice that would enable us to draw near to God for ourselves.

WHY THE NEED FOR JESUS' SACRIFICE?

The idea that God allowed his Son to be offered as a sacrifice, and did so in such a bloody, horrific manner, is scorned by unbelievers, who cannot reconcile such a crude idea with a loving, heavenly Father. Comprehending the awesome right-eousness of our holy God isn't easy even for Christians, so it's understandable how apparently impossible it is for hearts still blinded to the reality that God even exists. Nevertheless, the fact remains that God's perfect holiness necessitates an atoning sacrifice for our sin before we can be reconciled to him.

We are made in the image of God; the shed blood of animals would always be inadequate for such atonement. The condition of perfection that is necessary in order to be fully acceptable and reconciled to God could only be achieved through the blood of the perfect Lamb. Only this divine act of grace in the gift of God's Son provides the necessary inward cleansing of conscience that unites us with our holy Father—a sacrifice made once and for ever to purify the core of our being.

Indeed, when Jesus cried out from the cross, 'It is finished!' the curtain in the temple that separated the Most Holy Place from the people was torn in two—tangible evidence that the spiritual gateway to God's presence had been opened for all who would put their faith in his Son's sacrifice for their sins.

WHAT IS OUR RESPONSE?

'God so loved the world that he gave his one and only Son, that whoever believes in him shall not perish but have eternal life' (John 3:16). We each have a choice to believe that we are exiled from a relationship with our heavenly Father God and a choice to accept the Lamb of God as the only way by which our sin can be removed and the relationship restored. It is a gift. There is nothing we can do of ourselves to earn God's forgiveness and cleansing from sin.

Once we have accepted this necessary sacrifice and appreciated its implications, we find ourselves in a position of seeming inadequate thanksgiving for Christ's overwhelming love, evidenced by his inordinate suffering on our behalf.

Furthermore, we are the means to spread this essential message among our family and friends, a message explained in words but evidenced through the ongoing transformation of our attitudes, priorities and behaviour as God's Holy Spirit continues to bear his fruit through our lives.

Let's reflect on the suffering of the Lamb of God as we recognise our need of a Saviour. Let's take ample time for our hearts to express a depth of thanksgiving that supersedes words and let's seek to know our resurrected Lord in ever-increasing measure through the word and the Holy Spirit.

Since we have confidence to enter the Most Holy Place by the blood of Jesus… and since we have a great priest over the house of God, let us draw near to God with a sincere heart, in full assurance of faith, having our hearts sprinkled to cleanse us from a guilty conscience and having our bodies washed with pure water.

Let us hold unswervingly to the hope we profess, for he who promised is faithful. And let us consider how we may spur one another on toward love and good deeds. (Hebrews 10:19, 21–24)

TAKE IT FURTHER

Reflect

When we are sanctified—that is, made holy through Christ's atoning death—we are subsequently called to be holy (1 Corinthians 1:2), set apart from the attitudes, behaviour and perspectives of a world that denies God's existence. We cannot make ourselves holy in God's sight, as holiness is obtainable only through Christ's blood, but we can seek to bring him pleasure through dedicated, obedient, adoring hearts and lives, nurturing and taking care of his gift of divine relationship and eternal life. It is only out of the depths of gratitude for the Lamb of God, who was sacrificed on behalf of our sin, that a sincere desire to please our resurrected Saviour wells up within.

Pray

Lord Jesus, once again I am brought to my knees in humble recognition of my life, ingrained with sin, and of what you have so willingly done for me. I thank you; I love you; I worship you.

Read

Hebrews 7:18–28; 9:1—10:18

JESUS:
THE LIFE

When I celebrated my 40th birthday, I received a number of corny, derogatory, nostalgic and hilarious cards, including the familiar proclamations that at last 'life begins'. (Mind you, I've recently heard it said that 60 is the new 40, so I'll leave that up to you to decide!)

As it happens, my birthday did coincide with a period of reflection and an unusual number of life-changes, but it is not unusual to hope that life may take a turn for the better as we pass another birthday. If the previous year has worn us down with more than its fair share of difficulties, if we feel that we've slipped into an unfulfilling or unfruitful rut, or if we sense that God is guiding us in a new direction, the days following our birthday may be filled with longings for something new.

Furthermore, we may be waiting on a pay rise, longing for the outcome of an unresolved situation, relying on a proposal to come our way, seeking a new home or alternative employment or counting down the days to retirement.

There is nothing wrong with harbouring hopes or aspirations, but if we put too much emphasis on those desires, or if they remain out of reach, we can begin to feel as if life has been put on hold and, in turn, start to feel discouraged. We can keep going through the motions of our daily routines but may feel that our sense of purpose, happiness or fulfilment depends upon and waits until that desire has been fully satisfied, surpassed by a more favourable alternative or proven to be a non-starter. That certainly isn't what God intended when he created us to 'live and move and have our being' in him (Acts 17:28).

Jesus declared, 'I have come that they may have life, and have it to the full' (John 10:10) and he wasn't referring just to a future hope, but to experiencing life in its fullness today.

It sounds great in theory, doesn't it? But if we don't feel it has materialised in our present experience, we may be wondering why Christ's promise seems to have passed us by.

Let's consider what Jesus meant.

THE MEANING OF LIFE

Jesus said, 'I am… the life' (John 14:6), but he wasn't just affirming his role in breathing life into creation—which, of course, he did (John 1:1–4). Nor was he only pointing towards the future, when perfection will be restored and we'll be raised to new life in heaven—which is also true (Colossians 3:4). Jesus was talking about encountering eternal life right now, experiencing his infusion of spiritual life unbound by physical restrictions, enhancing our days in this world with the vitality, quality, power, provision and purpose of life that God intended.

Christ's life in us does not promise physical longevity,

material comfort or speedy resolution of problems—ideals that may be the height of some people's aspirations. Jesus promised so much more, both now and for the future.

He taught that 'life does not consist in the abundance of possessions... Life is more than food, and the body more than clothes' (Luke 12:15, 23). This doesn't imply that all Christians are supposed to live a life of austere, ascetic abstinence. I enjoy a trip to the shops to buy a new outfit and I appreciate the comforts of my home. I feel contented in the company of loved ones and satisfied by a job well done.

Nevertheless, Jesus pointed out that all these possessions and pursuits, and the things that make us feel fulfilled, should never be our basis of life, our primary goal, our sole source of well-being or motivation. After all, these things are only temporary; they often prove disappointing, short-lived, inadequate or unstable.

THE FOCUS OF LIFE

Rather, Christ is our life. He is our primary source of peace, contentment, purpose, encouragement and hope. If only we would set our hearts fully on our relationship with him rather than letting other aspects of life take over, we would experience what he really meant about giving us 'life to the full'.

It only takes the reading of a challenging biography such as that of Brother Yun, who suffered years of brutal persecution at the hands of Chinese officials, for us to appreciate believers who know what it means to live a superabundant life in Christ, no matter what their circumstances. We may or may not be called to endure such extremes, but such testimonies highlight our need to focus on our life in Christ more than we focus on the life of this world.

THE CHOICE OF LIFE

We have a choice. We can ignore Jesus' instruction and continue to focus our primary attention on realising our goals or we can reorganise our priorities and focus our primary attention on our relationship with him, seeking to live our physical life in the perspective of eternity.

I don't know how that will look for you in practice; I only know that I have a personal responsibility to set aside my own agenda and concentrate on Jesus, knowing that his life in me will work out God's loving purposes as he sees fit—and in so doing he will fulfil me beyond anything that this world has to offer.

Meanwhile, when we feel more inclined towards our hopes for this world or when the busy routine distracts us from his life, let's recall Christ's incredible promise: 'Seek first his kingdom and his righteousness, and all these things will be given to you as well' (Matthew 6:33). If we really believe that his promise is true, then surely those words are all we need to spur our hearts on in his direction.

HOW TO EMBRACE THE LIFE JESUS PROMISES US

Seek his guidance

You have made known to me the path of life; you will fill me with joy in your presence, with eternal pleasures at your right hand. (Psalm 16:11)

Have you ever been asked for directions, then watched as the thankful driver moves away but takes the opposite direction to the one you advised?

If we are privileged to have access to God's word, then we have a treasure of a book to provide guidance and purpose for life: where we have come from, where we are going, how we should live, what we should prioritise, how to relate to others and, of course, how to relate to God. Furthermore, we have God's word—his promise—regarding all sorts of matters, which we know he will not break.

But are we sometimes like that driver, asking for guidance but either forgetting it immediately or deciding that we think we know better? We can't expect to receive the 'superabundant life' that Christ promised if we then decide to live in the way we prefer.

So how about choosing to commit more time to reading and reflecting on God's word, asking the Holy Spirit to show us how we can apply it to our lives and then responding by putting what we've learnt into practice. When we do that, we can rest assured that God will fulfil his promise (Numbers 23:19).

Do not merely listen to the word, and so deceive yourselves. Do what it says... Those who look intently into the perfect law that gives freedom, and continue to do this, not forgetting what they have heard, but doing it—they will be blessed in what they do. (James 1:22, 25)

Submit to him

Delight yourself in the Lord and he will give you the desires of your heart. (Psalm 37:4)

Jesus promised to give us what he would define as a 'super-abundant life', but I recognise that we may harbour a deep yearning for something, or someone, that may or may not be what Jesus wants us to have. I also know how difficult, even impossible, it can be to let those desires go if we feel prompted to do so. In fact, we may not even want to surrender something that seems so very attractive or important to us.

But if we believe in Jesus' promise to give us 'life in all its fullness', then we do need to submit to what he knows is best. If we are struggling, let's not focus on that specific act of surrender, but let's focus on our relationship with him.

As the psalmist says, let's 'delight' ourselves in Jesus. Let's appreciate what he does for us; let's savour his promises; let's rejoice in praise and worship and take time to bask in his presence.

As we turn our hearts to Jesus—as we remain in him

(John 15:4)—so he pours his heart into ours. His desires become our desires and his promise to bring them about will subsequently be fulfilled. His promise to give us 'life' will be our tangible experience, and somehow the 'want' that we found so hard to give up gently slips out of our open hearts.

May he give you the desire of your heart and make all your plans succeed. (Psalm 20:4)

Pray

Teach me, O Lord, to follow your decrees… Turn my heart towards your statutes and not towards selfish gain. Turn my eyes away from worthless things; preserve my life according to your word. Fulfil your promise to your servant, so that you may be feared. (Psalm 119:33, 36–38)

JESUS:
LIGHT OF THE WORLD

The prophet Isaiah foretold that God would send the light of his presence to his people (Isaiah 9:2; 42:6; 49:6) and, approximately 700 years later, Jesus declared in the Jerusalem temple, 'I am the light of the world. Whoever follows me will never walk in darkness, but will have the light of life' (John 8:12). I wonder, however, if the analogy to light fails to inspire our relationship with Christ as readily as images of the counsellor or shepherd.

If so, then let's bear in mind that knowing Jesus as the light does not refer so much to the character whom we relate to as the atmosphere in which we live—energised and illuminated by his presence.

JESUS, THE LIGHT OF LIFE

Light is fundamental for life. In fact, I vividly recall my biology teacher explaining, in her usual exuberant, passionate style, the 'fascinating' process of photosynthesis—the means by which plants obtain energy, and therefore life, from light.

We were all given two glass jam jars, blotting paper and

two broad beans. Inserting the beans into the jars between the rolled-up paper and glass, we added a dash of water before placing one jar on a sunny windowsill and the other in a dark cupboard. (Apologies if I fail to exude the same excitement as my teacher!)

A few lessons later, we noted how the beans on the windowsill grew strong green shoots and creamy roots, then flowered and produced further seed. The beans left in the dark, however, struggled to produce only a few pallid, emaciated spindles before dying without even flowering. That image has stuck with me as I consider life lived in the light of Christ.

Jesus didn't intend for us to struggle in our spiritual development, but came so that we might experience the power and vitality of his life. To do so, we need to keep ourselves in the light of his presence, just as beans need to be kept in the sunlight in order to grow and seed.

Paul taught further on this subject when he encouraged the Ephesians to 'live as children of light (for the fruit of the light consists in all goodness, righteousness and truth)' (Ephesians 5:8–9). We can't expect to grow or enjoy a fruitful spiritual life, to experience the ever-increasing transformation into his likeness (2 Corinthians 3:18) or the full measure of Christ within (Ephesians 4:13), unless we remain in the presence of his light and seek to live by his ways.

I know fairly quickly when I've taken myself outside the light of his presence, be that through wilful rebellion or the conviction of unintentional sin, and it's a horrid place to be. When I'm done with exhausting myself by trying to justify my behaviour, I'm left with the cold, dark misery of a barren prayer life, uninspired work, tetchy attitudes toward others, lack of fulfilment or an oppressive burden haranguing my emotions—that which we call condemnation.

There are times when I actually sit and fester in this dark place of the soul—unwilling to let go of my self-satisfying traits or too proud to confess that I've been wrong. But while coming back into the light of Christ's presence (through sincere, heartfelt confession) is a humbling, soul-searching, even sacrificial experience, it is always accompanied by Christ's unconditional love, relief from oppressive guilt, the washing of forgiveness and the healing balm of grace.

'Whoever lives by the truth comes into the light' (John 3:21). We each have a choice to accept the truth that Jesus is the Messiah and, as we do so, the divine light of his life infuses eternal life to our spirits. But we also have a choice then to live by that truth—placing ourselves, as it were, on the sunny windowsill rather than remaining in the cupboard, living our lives in the light of Christ's presence instead of the ways of darkness. It's only as we put his teaching into practice that the full potential of Christ's vitality can energise, empower and bear fruit, in and through our lives.

JESUS, THE LIGHT TO LIVE BY

Light is aptly defined in my dictionary as 'the medium of illumination that makes sight possible'.

If you've ever been caught doing something wrong, you'll know how you wished you could have turned off the light. But if you ever try cleaning out a dusty, dirty attic strewn with spiders' webs and mouse droppings, you'll appreciate the help of an electric bulb. If you ever try to study from a comprehensive textbook, you'll appreciate a decent desk lamp. If you ever try walking in the dark along an isolated country lane, you'll appreciate the guidance of a torch. And if you ever feel the gut-wrenching fear of darkness, you'll appreciate the comfort of a nightlight.

Similarly, the world in which we live is steeped in spiritual darkness that enshrouds our lives with sin, confusion, lack of direction, hopelessness, fear, isolation and so on. But Jesus, the light of the world, brings both life and illumination into this barren shadow of spiritual death—light that imparts righteousness, truth, clarity, revelation, guidance, direction, hope, comfort and reassurance. While the interaction of light with the retina in the eye enables us to see, so the contact of Christ's light with our souls enlightens the eyes of our hearts (Ephesians 1:17–18).

We can choose to stumble around in the darkness relying on our limited opinions, abilities and physical senses to do what we feel is right, to fathom the infinite depths of scripture, to choose what we think is best for our lives and seek solace or satisfaction in the company of the fickle, temporary attractions of the world. But consider how that wastes the potential resources made available to us in the light of Christ's presence.

If we take the time to pause—to pray, to listen, to read God's word—the presence of Christ's light will surely guide the way far better than our own intuition. Furthermore, it will comfort us when the going gets tough, encouraging us to persevere rather than give up.

I hope this brief reflection on Christ as the light of the

world is helpful, but we can't quite leave it there, for as much as we are empowered and led by his light, we also have a responsibility to share it with others.

YOU ARE THE LIGHT OF THE WORLD

Jesus described John the Baptist as a lamp that gave light (John 5:35), born into his generation for the unique purpose of pointing others to Jesus and revealing who Jesus was. We too are lamps, filled with the light of the life of Christ by his Holy Spirit so that others may see and recognise him for themselves.

This astounding truth begs the question, what are we doing with our lamps? If we're seeking to live in the light of Christ's presence, our lamps will indeed be bright as they reflect his glory—but with whom are we sharing that light? Are we trying to hide our lamps within our home, church and circle of Christian friends, or beneath a cloak of compromise? Or are we lamps with legs—taking Christ's light into the world to shine before others, 'that they may see [our] good deeds and praise [our] Father in heaven' (Matthew 5:16)?

Our lamp will shine Christ's light into the spiritual darkness where we live, work and socialise; its purity will contrast with the impurity of sinful behaviour; its truth will counter deceit; its comfort will reassure those in despair; its hue of grace will offer hope to a culture striving for love, acceptance and success. Moreover, it will reveal the person of Jesus.

We cannot force people to accept him; in fact, some will prefer the life lived in darkness (John 3:19). Others, however, who recognise our fulfilment and purpose in life, our genuine sincerity, integrity and love and our peace in difficult circumstances, and are attracted by the confidence we have for today and for the future, might well perceive Christ's light in the darkness and ask us the question, 'What is it that's different about you?'

Each one of us is unique. We all have different experiences, upbringings, characters, genes, skills, interests and relationships. But if we've accepted Jesus as Lord, we all share the same life-giving light. Let's determine to remain in that light and so let it shine brightly in our particular place in the world.

TAKE IT FURTHER

Reflect

What challenges you?

- Have you accepted Jesus as your personal Saviour and Lord? If so, would you consider that you've grown spiritually over the last six months—that your relationship with Jesus has deepened and your submission to his ways has been refined?
- Are you prone to racing into decisions, responsibilities or simply the routine of your day without first focusing on Jesus and what he might want to say or do?

- How obvious and accessible is the lamp of your life to people who've yet to know Jesus themselves?

Pray

Lord Jesus, I'm reminded that you didn't merely describe yourself as the light, but you possess the very qualities of light that I need, to grow spiritually, to follow your ways and your paths, and to reveal you to other people. Please show me the ways by which I step into the shadows, thereby diminishing the brightness of your life in me.

Read

John 1:1–13; 8:12–30; Ephesians 4:17—5:21; 1 John 1: 5–10

JESUS:
THE LIVING STONE

Picture in your mind's eye a stone building. You can't see the foundation, of course, but it's there: a solid, secure platform on which the building stands. At the base of the junction of two walls sits the most significant stone in the whole structure—the cornerstone—which anchors, aligns and determines the entire image and bearing of the building. The walls are built from many stones, each unique in its colour and shape, yet all dovetailed together by the expert hands of a skilful stonemason.

With this in mind, let's recall a verse from scripture: 'Come to him, the living Stone' (1 Peter 2:4). When Jesus calls himself 'the good shepherd', he invites us into the protective presence of his loving, guiding, nurturing care. When Jesus describes himself as 'the door', he beckons us to take a step of faith and walk right through into the kingdom of God. But how do we relate to Christ as 'the living Stone'? Stone, after all, is an inorganic mineral—the hard, compact, lifeless matter from which cliffs and mountains are made.

A single stone, however, isn't supposed to be considered in isolation; rather, we are to broaden our thinking to something much larger—the construction of a building made up of many stones. Jesus applied this analogy to himself (Mark 12:10; quoting Psalm 118:22), then Paul and Peter took up the theme. But we read about it first in the Old Testament.

'This is what the Sovereign Lord says,' Isaiah declared to God's people: '"See, I lay a stone in Zion, a tested stone, a precious cornerstone for a sure foundation; the one who trusts will never be dismayed"' (Isaiah 28:16). Initially, that stone was laid quite literally, as the cornerstone of the temple in Jerusalem, the dwelling-place of God among his people. Ultimately, however, Isaiah's messianic prophecy was fulfilled in Jesus Christ. Jesus is the definitive sanctuary for the Holy Spirit—'tested' and proven to offer reliable promises into which we might dovetail and build our lives; 'precious' because of Christ's unparalleled role in the divine plan of salvation; the 'cornerstone' from which the spiritual dwelling of God forms and takes shape; a 'sure foundation', a solid, unshakeable rock on which that dwelling stands.

This, then, is the one with whom we engage when we come to Jesus, 'the living Stone'. It's Christ who establishes, orientates and builds a spiritual dwelling in the hearts of Christian believers as they join together, in him, as the sanctuary for the Holy Spirit, also known as his Church.

This edifice isn't made of lifeless bricks and mortar, no matter how appealing the exterior design and interior décor of our local 'church' buildings may be. Rather, it's a living construction, built by Jesus who provides its foundation (1 Corinthians 3:11) and the chief cornerstone (Ephesians 2:20): he is the living Stone (1 Peter 2:4).

THE FOUNDATION STONE

For no one can lay any foundation other than the one already laid, which is Jesus Christ. (1 Corinthians 3:11)

Any structure built to last requires a solid foundation, and those constructed for significant buildings in biblical times were made of stone, none being so important as the large, quality blocks used to provide a foundation of dressed stone for the Jerusalem temple (1 Kings 5:17).

A spiritual building needs foundations, too, and the promised Messiah is the only 'stone' we can use (Isaiah 28:16). But as much as we may already know that in our minds, there are times when we need to remind our hearts that the foundation for building his Church is not based on our activities, good works, a preferred style of worship or any other such thing. There is only one foundation upon which God will build and that is 'the author and perfecter of our faith' (Hebrews 12:2), who shares his Father's awesome passion for the unsaved; the one who revealed God's eternal love for his people and whose sacrificial obedience on the cross paid the price to save us from our sins and Satan's dominion of death. It is only as we accept him as our Saviour and surrender to him as Lord of our lives in thought, word and deed that we build upon the right foundation.

THE CHIEF CORNERSTONE

Consequently, you are… members of God's household… with Christ Jesus himself as the chief cornerstone. In him, the whole building is joined together and rises to become a holy temple in the Lord. (Ephesians 2:19–21)

The cornerstone is the most significant stone in any building, and both Isaiah and Paul remind us that Jesus is the chief cornerstone of God's home among his people. Direction and unity in the building work will never come from an attempt to propagate a human point of view, but it will arise when each of us dovetails into the cornerstone—into Christ's holy ways and Christ's righteous purposes.

The shape and orientation of the Church is not determined by the type of organisation we are, by following ritual or tradition, the use of liturgy or the lack of it, the playing of an organ or a guitar and drums—but by Jesus Christ. Where Christ is, there is his Church and there is both the foundation and the alignment for building God's dwelling-place on earth.

This cornerstone anchors the building in truth and orientates the building in holiness. Does that reflect the bearing of the spiritual building in which we play our part?

THE LIVING STONE

In him you too are being built together to become a dwelling in which God lives by his Spirit. (Ephesians 2:22)

We've considered our solid foundation and we've set in place our cornerstone, but God's building needs some walls —and to build those we come to Christ, 'the living Stone'.

Only Jesus can provide the life and energy for the construction of God's spiritual building, but, as we receive that life, you and I also become like living stones (1 Peter 2:4–5).

It is by coming together as believers in the Lord Jesus Christ, whether on a Sunday or during the week, that we effectively build God's spiritual house—and not from bricks and mortar, but from living stones, each individual believer being joined together with other believers in its ongoing construction.

It's what we might describe as an amorphous edifice— one without the permanent shape of buildings made from 'dead' stones but with the changing dimensions of God's assembled people, his Church, as each new stone takes its place in the structure.

And so, in keeping with the emphasis throughout the New Testament, it's in our coming together as believers that we shall experience his power in greater measure, joined together in Christ as the dwelling-place of God.

WHAT IS OUR RESPONSE?

The living Stone, the cornerstone and foundation of our faith, invites us to 'come to him', to draw near to God through an intimate relationship with Jesus. But do we? Is he our foundation and cornerstone, directing, designing and anchoring our lives? Or is he the stone that causes us to stumble (Isaiah 8:14; 1 Peter 2:8), the person in whom we feel unable to put our trust, the name that we have rejected? If the latter, then do please consider again Isaiah's message concerning that precious stone: 'the one who trusts will never be dismayed'.

If, however, you've received Christ's gift of eternal life, then join with me in also accepting our role as living stones. Let's link hearts, hands, minds and wills to the holy bearing of the cornerstone of our faith, standing firm on the only foundation of eternal life as we commit to corporate worship as God intended.

Jesus is infinitely more than an analogy to inorganic stone: he is the breath of life to our spirits. Without him we are 'dead' stones; without one another we cannot build God's spiritual dwelling on earth.

*

TAKE IT FURTHER

Reflect

In 1 Corinthians 6:19–20, Paul wrote about each individual believer being a temple of God's Spirit, but in 3:9–17, and elsewhere in the New Testament, he emphasised the need for believers to be joined together—to be united in Christ—in the ongoing construction of God's dwelling-place.

We each have a responsibility, therefore, to learn about and put into practice the principles of consecrating our lives as a holy temple, but personal devotion to Christ also includes corporate integration into his church.

Are you a believer but keeping your faith to yourself, pre-ferring your own mode of worship in the privacy of your home? Jesus longs that you would draw near to him, the living Stone, by means of joining with other Christians. Im-perfect as we all are, it is only as we join together in Christ that he can work in, and through, his church to the measure he intended.

Pray

Lord Jesus, please forgive me for the times I've treated 'church' as a place to offer a token act of service, simply to have my needs met or to come and go as I please. Thank you for the powerful, spiritual building you purposed for it to be. Please help me, Holy Spirit, to fulfil my part.

Read

1 Peter 2:4–12; 1 Corinthians 3:9–17; Mark 12:1–12; Romans 9:30–33

JESUS:
PRINCE OF PEACE

I love preparing for and celebrating Christmas, but I do wonder what people think when they receive a festive card picturing a dove or the stable scene, entitled 'Prince of Peace'. After all, with ongoing warring factions in the world, the turmoil of natural disasters, escalating gun and knife crime and breakdown of personal relationships, it doesn't take a genius to recognise that the promised 'Prince of Peace' is apparently yet to live up to his name.

No, it doesn't take a genius—it just takes faith to recognise that he does, in fact, fulfil that title.

It was the prophet Isaiah who heralded the name to be given to the promised Messiah (Isaiah 9:6). It's inevitable that rebellion against God's holy ways and purpose is going to reap consequences, but Isaiah brought hope to the people of Israel who were living in the darkness of exile from God's presence and favour. He promised forgiveness and restoration to God; first, when the exiles returned to Jerusalem, but more importantly, when the Prince of Peace brought the spiritual healing required for a people estranged from God by sin.

So we read how the angels praised God when that prince was born on earth: 'Glory to God in the highest, and on earth peace to those on whom his favour rests' (Luke 2:14). Nor did it end there. About 33 years later, people called out praises, too, as the prince rode into Jerusalem for the Passover celebrations: 'Many people spread their cloaks on the road, while others spread branches they had cut in the fields. Those who went ahead and those who followed shouted, "Hosanna! Blessed is he who comes in the name of the Lord! Blessed is the coming kingdom of our father David! Hosanna in the highest!"' (Mark 11:8–10).

But their royal tributes and praises changed to 'Crucify!' when, a few days later, the Prince of Peace didn't meet them on their own terms. They'd heralded the leader they thought would bring peace from Roman oppression, but Jesus revealed that his kingdom wasn't of this world; it was from another place (John 18:36). They misunderstood Christ's reign, and it's not so very different today.

When our non-believing friends receive 'Prince of Peace' Christmas cards or find themselves at a carol service, singing 'Hark! The herald angels sing... Peace on earth...' they too may dismiss the prince who hasn't brought the peace that they expected. But scripture isn't referring to temporary reconciliation between nations or some kind of external tranquillity. Rather, it speaks of the peace we find with God when we put our faith in Christ. This was what Isaiah and the angels were referring to—the depth of spiritual peace that pervades body, mind and soul through relationship with the Messiah.

JESUS' GIFT TO US

If you are reading this study around Christmas time, some of you may be about to face your first Christmas away from home, your first Christmas for many years without your spouse, or your first (or fifth, or tenth) Christmas wondering how your finances are going to stretch to meet December's expectations; you may be fearing the sense of 'aloneness' that the season can accentuate or wishing it was all over as you battle with your health.

Our concerns for war-torn and impoverished communities, our anxieties for family or friends, our personal hurts and disappointments, are just a few ways in which this fallen world might influence the reality of Christ's peace in our hearts. We're not the first to feel like this.

The disciples felt unsettled by growing hostilities towards their Master, who was determined to face his enemy head-on. So, by the evening of the last supper, tensions were high as Jesus spoke of his impending departure. Nevertheless, he left his intimate friends with the promise of an awesome parting gift: 'Peace I leave with you; my peace I give you. I do not give to you as the world gives. Do not let your hearts be troubled and do not be afraid' (John 14:27).

After the resurrection came the fulfilment of that promise: 'On the evening of that first day of the week, when the disciples were together, with the doors locked for fear of the Jews, Jesus came and stood among them and said, "Peace be with you!" … And with that he breathed on them and said, "Receive the Holy Spirit"' (John 20:19, 22).

The Prince of Peace did, and does, live up to his name.

Jesus—perfect and at one with his Father throughout his mortal life—continues to impart that wholeness and spiritual well-being to modern-day disciples. It's an eternal peace that the world most certainly cannot give, the inner rest that a believer finds in fellowship with God.

Jesus is the Prince of Peace, the prince of a kingdom not of this world but a kingdom that is within you and me as we place our trust in him (Luke 17:21). It's a very real and present peace, reserved only for those 'on whom his favour rests'—on those with faith in his salvation.

Perhaps you've yet to open your heart to Jesus and receive the promised blessing of his kingdom's peace. If so, why not pause right now, confess that you need Jesus to forgive the life you've led independently of him and ask him by his Spirit to come into your heart.

Perhaps you already know the Prince of Peace, but the impact of this fallen world overshadows your spiritual well-being. If so, then pause now and ask him to breathe his Spirit afresh on your life; open your heart in expectation and take, or make, time—quality time—to draw closer to his presence. Feeling distanced or separated from God causes inevitable anguish, but, in the same way that the resurrection removed all doubt and fear from the disciples' hearts, so the living Prince of Peace still longs to heal your inner being, too.

OUR GIFT TO OTHERS

As we accept Christ's gift to us this Christmas time, remember that it's not only to be received, but also to be shared, as we live out its implications.

Jesus, by his Spirit, imparts peace into every believer and, likewise, we're to keep in step with his Spirit, so sharing that peace with others. 'Make every effort to live in peace with everyone… See to it that no one misses the grace of God and that no bitter root grows up to cause trouble and defile many' (Hebrews 12:14–15).

The spiritual fruit of a life lived for and with Jesus is peace (Galatians 5:22), the inner harmony that our relationship with God expresses to our neighbour, no matter the stresses and strains of life that seek to snatch it away. Indeed, our natural tendency is towards irritability, panic, bitterness or anger: even the manic rush of Christmas can challenge our inward peace. But we are obliged to exercise faith and allow our prince's peace to pervade our lives. And perhaps, as we do so, our non-believing friends will look at their 'Prince of Peace' Christmas cards and turn their thoughts to us—a people of peace, love and inward security, who reflect and impart Christ's reign today.

TAKE IT FURTHER

Reflect

'Do not suppose that I have come to bring peace to the earth. I did not come to bring peace, but a sword. For I have come to turn "a man against his father, a daughter against her mother, a daughter-in-law against her mother-in-law—a man's enemies will be the members of his own household."' (Matthew 10:34–36)

Isaiah 9:5–7 and Luke 2:14 confirm Jesus' mission to restore peace between human beings and God where that relationship had been broken by sin. Ironically, however, that peace will itself cause conflict as our differing personal responses to him divide our opinions, outlook and purpose—regrettable but inevitable, even between family members.

In Jesus, however, we have a new family bond with fellow believers—one that we can nurture now and enjoy for eternity.

Praise

Hark! The herald angels sing:
'Glory to the new-born King.
Peace on earth, and mercy mild,
God and sinners reconciled!'…

Hail the heaven-born Prince of Peace!
Hail, the Sun of righteousness!
Light and life to all he brings,
Risen with healing in his wings…

Hark! the herald angels sing:
'Glory to the new-born King.'
CHARLES WESLEY (1707–88)

Read

Isaiah 9:1–7; Luke 1:68–79; 2:8–14; John 14:22–31

JESUS:
OUR PROTECTOR

Wouldn't it be marvellous if, on our profession of faith in Jesus Christ, we received divine protection from trouble and difficulty? In reality, however, our ongoing experience as Christ's disciples proves that we'll never be completely protected from the consequences of living in a fallen world.

We suffer physical pain, heartache, anxiety, trauma, discouragement and grief, resulting perhaps from relationship breakdown, financial insecurity, health concerns, religious persecution, victimisation, abuse, natural disasters, accident and countless other difficulties encountered in this life.

Many of us can testify how Jesus has intervened to alleviate a particular problem, but he never said he would shield us from them all. He is merciful, compassionate and constantly present, but he said that we would have trouble (John 16:33). Although we are children of God, we continue to live in a world that is under the influence of Satan—our adversary, the father of lies, a murderer and deceiver.

As much as we might like an easygoing life, it is a greater relief that God has not abandoned us to Satan's activities. Indeed, in 2 Thessalonians 3:3, Paul calls Jesus our protector —the one who defends us against evil spirits, our hope for eternity and our refuge for today.

Satan had no hold on Jesus' perfect life (John 14:30). Consequently, our enemy's power over the human spirit was defeated when Jesus conquered death on our behalf, but we do have to ask Christ's forgiveness for living independently of God and trust him as our only means of gaining eternal life. Until we do so, we remain under the influence of the evil one (1 John 5:19).

This does not imply that every unbeliever is demonically possessed! But it does mean that the ownership of their spirit remains under the authority of the prince of this world, the god of this age, rather than their loving heavenly Father (2 Corinthians 4:4).

When we confess Jesus as Lord, however, he protects our spirits in him for ever. After all, Satan has no control or power over Jesus, so, when we ask the Lord to come into our lives by his Spirit, we are kept safe and need have no fear of death. In this life we may have to endure physical hardship, but spiritually we cannot be harmed (1 John 5:18).

Meanwhile, and until the day Satan is cast into an eternal hell, he seeks to hinder, confuse and ravage the outworking of God's loving rule and purpose through the lives of his beloved people. But Jesus, our protector, is ever present to strengthen and defend us.

In certain environments, our physical bodies require special protection and we would be foolish not to equip ourselves accordingly—wearing a coat, scarf and gloves in wintry weather, sun cream on a hot day, a helmet when riding a motorbike or a bulletproof vest in the army.

Similarly, while living in the environment of Satan's dominion of evil, we require the protection of Jesus Christ against the enemy's strategies to influence us as part of his attack against God. After all, 'our struggle is not against flesh and blood, but against the rulers, against the authorities, against the powers of this dark world and against the spiritual forces of evil in the heavenly realms' (Ephesians 6:12).

Simply being alive in this world is to be part of a spiritual battle between God and his enemy. Certainly, we may sense the oppression of spiritual attack more keenly in certain circumstances, but we still need spiritual protection each and every day.

Satan not only blinds the minds of unbelievers to the saving grace of the gospel (2 Corinthians 4:4), but will also try to tempt, manipulate, influence or distract our behaviour in order to promote his ungodly ways rather than God's righteous purposes.

He wants us to grow bitter rather than forgive, to hate rather than love, to act selfishly in place of seeking the good of other people and to succumb to greed in place of self-control. He will also sow seeds of mistrust in God's infallible promises.

We each have a personal responsibility to choose God's ways rather than give in to evil temptations, but Christ offers his own protection to help us stand firm—protection that Paul likens to spiritual armour (Ephesians 6:10–18).

Throughout his letter to the Ephesian church, Paul taught about living life 'in Christ' (1:3; 2:10; 4:32) and concluded by saying, 'Be strong in the Lord' (6:10). This strength, he explained, arises from receiving Christ's protection—from wearing, as Paul describes it, 'the armour of God'.

Putting on our spiritual protection is not akin to getting

dressed in front of the mirror, putting on woolly scarf, helmet or bulletproof vest. Rather, it is a matter of living within our protection, living life 'in Christ'.

Are we allowing the enemy a foothold (Ephesians 4:27) by giving in to his temptation and lies, then permitting him to multiply the effects in and through our lives—for example, fostering bitterness instead of forgiveness, pursuing selfish ambition instead of seeking the best for others, or criticising rather than encouraging? Or are we living our lives with a conscious dependence on Jesus' means of spiritual protection? Are we choosing to live by the ways of his Spirit, thereby resisting the enemy's taunts and shielding ourselves from his condemnation by standing firm 'in Christ'?

HOW TO WEAR THE ARMOUR OF GOD

Put on the full armour of God so that you can take your stand against the devil's schemes… so that when the day of evil comes, you may be able to stand your ground. (Ephesians 6:11, 13)

- 'The belt of truth buckled around your waist' (v. 14): The width and thickness of the leather belts encircling Roman soldiers' waists protected their kidneys from enemy swords and were essential for attaching the remaining armour. Likewise, Christ protects us from succumbing to enemy attacks, enabling us to stand against them as we live within the truth of his word—not just reading it but aligning the way that we live to his holy instruction. Furthermore, it's the 'belt of truth' that enables us to 'wear' the rest of God's armour.

- 'The breastplate of righteousness in place' (v. 14): The Roman soldier protected his heart with chainmail or metal-plated armour, and our hearts are protected from Satan's accusations as we seek to live in step with the ways of the Spirit.

  We shall all do things wrong and Satan will try to condemn us, but we have been given the protection of Christ's perfect righteousness, which the enemy cannot touch. So, as we seek to align our lives with his righteousness, sincerely repenting of the things we do wrong, we can stand against the enemy with confidence, defeating every discouraging accusation he hurls at us.

- 'Your feet fitted with the readiness that comes from the gospel of peace' (v. 15): Roman soldiers wore studded boots to give them a solid grip when fighting in muddy or uneven terrain and wielding a heavy sword. Provided we trust in the truth of the gospel message of Jesus and his unconditional love, we too can stand upright when the enemy tries to trip us up, perhaps by tempting us to seek God's approval through good works, rote prayers or Bible knowledge.

- 'Take up the shield of faith' (v. 16): The structure of the Roman shield was resilient to arrows that had been set alight before being launched. Satan's legions of evil spirits also launch fiery arrows in the guise of criticism, spiteful words or unjust acts, for instance. If we allow them to penetrate our hearts, they can ignite fear, discouragement, anger, unforgiveness, vengeance and so on. But as we take up our shield of faith in Christ, trusting in and living out his loving, righteous ways, we shall remain in his protection as we extinguish the flames before they are able to penetrate.

- 'Take the helmet of salvation' (v. 17): Head protection is vital in any battle, including the one we face daily against our spiritual foe. Satan will try to penetrate the truth of our salvation with lies. But, just as the Roman helmet was so tightly secured that no one could remove it, so Satan has no power to snatch our salvation. Christ gives it to us and no one can take it from us. We must receive it, accepting its truths in defence against Satan's deceit and discouragement, and fixing our thoughts on Jesus so that we will not grow weary and lose heart (Hebrews 3:1; 12:3).
- 'Take... the sword of the Spirit' (v. 17): Finally, as the Roman had his weapon, we have been given the sword of the Spirit—the word of God that the Holy Spirit will inspire to our hearts for each occasion. Jesus used the word to slay every temptation that Satan hurled at him in the wilderness, and we too have a powerful defence as we follow his example. But, as its full description suggests, we cannot pull out any scripture at will; we must wait for the Spirit's direction in order to empower our 'sword'.

Read

2 Thessalonians 3:1–5; 1 John 5:13–21; Ephesians 6:10–18

JESUS:
THE RESURRECTION AND THE LIFE

Picture the scene. Lazarus was dead. He had been entombed in a cave for four days by the time Jesus arrived, the warm, stagnant Mediterranean air hastening decay (John 11:39).

'I am the resurrection and the life,' Jesus counselled Martha. 'Those who believe in me will live, even though they die' (v. 25). Then he proceeded to command Lazarus to come out of the tomb.

'The dead man came out, his hands and feet wrapped with strips of linen, and a cloth around his face. Jesus said to them, "Take off the grave clothes and let him go"' (v. 44). Imagine your reaction on seeing a supposed 'dead man' walk out of his tomb—the shock, horror, amazement and awe on beholding the glory of God at work. Imagine the cries, the cheers, the sighs, the tears—and nothing on the air but the sweet fragrance of country life!

Now consider your response. Would you have passed it off as a scam, kept it to yourself or talked about it incessantly with everyone you subsequently met? Would you have rejected Jesus as a fraud or would you, too, have put your faith in him?

Picture another scene. The disciples shared bread and

wine with Jesus while he spoke of betrayal and death; they accompanied him to the garden to pray, but watched in fear as guards approached. They fled when they saw him arrested. They sobbed when they saw him a prisoner— barely recognisable from beatings, whippings, thorns and chains. All but John and a few of the women dissolved into the heaving crowds, spent of emotion, crushed in spirit, hopeless, desolate, broken.

As for those who remained to the end, they saw his bruised, broken, bleeding body nailed viciously to a cross. They heard his tormented cries to a silent Father. They watched that fateful rise of his chest as he gasped his final breath.

The corpse was wrapped in spices and linen, then laid in a nearby tomb.

On the evening of that first day of the week, when the disciples were together, with the doors locked for fear of the Jews, Jesus came and stood among them and said, 'Peace be with you!' After he said this, he showed them his hands and side. The disciples were overjoyed when they saw the Lord. Again Jesus said, 'Peace be with you! As the Father has sent me, I am sending you.' And with that he breathed on them and said, 'Receive the Holy Spirit.' (John 20:19–22)

Once again, imagine your own reaction to seeing your 'dead' beloved Lord appear in a room as living flesh and blood, his hands bearing the scars of crucifixion while he ate, drank and talked with his disciples. What would you feel—terror, astonishment, excitement, joy, gratitude, wonder, worship? And how would that inward reaction impact your outward response?

Jesus hadn't said to Martha, 'I will be' the resurrection, or even, 'I will give you the resurrection', but 'I am the resurrection and the life.' And he proved his claim unequivocally when divine power surged through his being, defeated the spiritual enemy and thereby conquered death, raising him for ever in a resurrected body.

Furthermore, Jesus had also counselled the grieving Martha, saying, 'Whoever lives and believes in me will never die. Do you believe this?' (11:26).

When Jesus returns and consummates his kingdom, we, who have been made spiritually alive through faith in his sacrificial death for the forgiveness of our sins, shall also be raised in a resurrected body to eternal life in God's glorious presence (1 Corinthians 15:20–23).

Paul writes, 'Don't you know that all of us who were baptised into Christ Jesus were baptised into his death? … If we have been united with him like this in his death, we will certainly also be united with him in his resurrection' (Romans 6:3, 5).

When Jesus raised Lazarus from the dead, Martha's grief was infused with resurrection hope, available to those who believe in Christ.

Moreover, encountering Jesus, 'the Resurrection and the Life', in that locked upper room not only filled the disciples with immense joy but also radically transformed the purpose and priorities of their lives. Filled with the Holy Spirit, they were no longer trapped in the violence, heartache, despondency and perceived failure of the 'Good Friday' world that had forsaken God. Their encounter with the risen Lord renewed their spirits, reconciled them to their heavenly Father, resourced them with kingdom power, authorised them to take their stand against the enemy and filled them with his divine presence through the coming of the Holy Spirit.

This life-changing encounter manifested itself not just inwardly, but outwardly, too. Fishermen turned orators, zealots turned peacemakers, secret disciples turned public evangelists, uneducated peasants turned teachers of scripture and fearful cowards turned bold witnesses. They were unconcerned by the hardships of life on the road for weeks on end with very little money, and undaunted by the threats of beatings, persecutions and martyrdom.

But what about us? As disciples of the Lord Jesus, have our lives been impacted by 'the Resurrection and the Life' in like manner? Or are we prone to enjoying the reflection, celebration, inspiration and renewal of our Easter celebrations, only to discard any ongoing response with the coloured foil from our chocolate eggs?

The Lord said through his messenger, 'These people come near to me with their mouth and honour me with their lips, but their hearts are far from me. Their worship of me is based on merely human rules which they have been taught' (Isaiah 29:13).

Ezekiel, too, berated the people who listened to God's words without responding to them in practice (Ezekiel 33:31–32), a theme taken up throughout the New Testament by Jesus, Paul and James among others (Luke 6:47–49; Philippians 4:9; 1 Timothy 5:4; James 1:22).

Indeed, the message of the cross and our meeting with 'the Resurrection and the Life' may become so familiar that they lose some of their impact. If this is true for you, or you feel you've settled into a comfortable religious rut, it's time to take action.

✳

HOW TO TAKE YOUR 'RESURRECTION ENCOUNTER' INTO THE REST OF YOUR LIFE

Build your faith

Praise be to the God and Father of our Lord Jesus Christ! In his great mercy he has given us new birth into a living hope through the resurrection of Jesus Christ from the dead. (1 Peter 1:3)

We have an incredible, indescribable eternity awaiting us, with a phenomenal empowering to fulfil our lives today. This is certainly something to be joyful and hopeful about. Let's start by taking time to build up our faith in thanksgiving and praise to God for making this possible, by sending us his Son Jesus, 'the Resurrection and the Life'.

Prepare your mind

Therefore, prepare your minds for action; be self-controlled; set your hope fully on the grace to be given you when Jesus Christ is revealed. (1 Peter 1:13)

In light of what we've been thanking and praising God for, think about the following questions.

- Are we prepared for action, ready to be doing something in response to our encounter with 'the Resurrection and the Life'? Are we in a state of readiness or, rather, one of reluctance, indisposition, disinclination or even opposition?

- An encounter with the purity and holiness of the risen Lord Jesus shows up all those habits, attitudes and secret sins that we try to bury from view. His cleansing is a free gift available to truly repentant hearts, but the ongoing impact of his forgiveness will only bear fruit as we then seek to honour, reflect and promote our encounter by keeping in step with the ways of the Holy Spirit living within.

- What are we setting our hopes on? If we work for, pursue, dream of or excessively aspire to the temporary things of today, our distraction could subtly overshadow and potentially devalue the true worth of our heavenly inheritance. Consequently, those pursuits and dreams may have greater impact on how we live than our encounter with Jesus does.

Be available

Paul said, 'I want to know Christ and the power of his resurrection' (Philippians 3:10a). Do we? Are we determined to become increasingly acquainted with Jesus in ever-deepening intimacy, familiarising ourselves with our Lord with greater understanding and perception, so that we may also experience the outflow of his resurrection exerted in our lives?

Take up your cross

I want to know… the fellowship of sharing in his sufferings, becoming like him in his death, and so, somehow, to attain to the resurrection from the dead. (vv. 10–11)

As someone once said, 'Friday always comes before Sunday. The trouble is, we want to have it the other way around.' Jesus said, 'Those who do not carry their cross and follow me cannot be my disciples' (Luke 14:27). We can believe in Jesus for salvation, but unless we're prepared to 'carry our cross' as well as receive the blessings of responding to our 'resurrection' encounter, we cannot be a disciple—cannot experience the full empowering of the resurrection today as the New Testament disciples did.

Do we want to be empowered by 'the Resurrection and the Life'? If so, let's respond to our encounter with him and dedicate ourselves afresh to being his disciple.

'Lord, may my personal encounter with you override all other motivations in my life.'

Read

John 11:1–46; Romans 6:1–14; 1 Corinthians 15:21–58

JESUS:
THE ROCK

When I was at junior school, I attended trampoline lessons, which took place in the sports hall at our local leisure centre. The air-conditioned, centrally heated atmosphere was warm, dusty and dry. The three-hour session of bouncing, seat-drops, back flips and somersaults, interspersed with constant nattering to my friends, guaranteed a raving thirst.

I have vivid memories of being driven back home, consumed by my need for a drink, and of racing through the door to fill glass after glass of cool, refreshing water. Nevertheless, my weekly exploits were worlds apart from the need for water that the Hebrews endured, every hour of every day, while traipsing through the Sinai desert.

God had promised to provide for his covenant people, but the Hebrews tended to grow disgruntled with their lot. They often grumbled or complained to Moses and Aaron that they preferred being in slavery, where they 'enjoyed' the fish, leeks and melons of Egypt.

They also grumbled about the lack of an abundant water supply—that a drink to satisfy their thirst wasn't always immediately available. Either their trust in God's promises had faltered or, like a demanding toddler, they were simply too impatient to wait and ranted relentlessly for what they wanted 'NOW!'

On two such occasions, near the beginning and the end of their desert sojourn, God provided the water they craved from a seemingly dry and barren rock (Exodus 17:3, 5–6; Numbers 20:2–3, 11).

God could have led them to an oasis or dropped a deluge from the sky, but I think his chosen method was rather poignant. After all, his people often called him their 'rock'—their powerful, reliable, implicitly trustworthy creator and provider (Deuteronomy 32:4,15; Psalm 18:2; 19:14; 40:2).

So God aptly reminded them of his faithfulness by using a rock to provide the life-giving water they required—a suitable prompt to remind them that their complaint was quite unnecessary as he already knew what they needed and would be sure to provide it. He hadn't led them out of Egypt simply to abandon them.

Let's consider what this has to say with regard to Jesus being 'the rock'—the spiritual rock from whom our life-giving supply of 'living water' flows unceasingly. 'They drank from the spiritual rock that accompanied them, and that rock was Christ' (1 Corinthians 10:4).

Water is essential to life. In fact, medical and nutritional experts state that, while the average person can live from four to six weeks without food, the body cannot survive without water for longer than three days.

Over 70 per cent of the human body is made up of water. Furthermore, it plays a fundamental role in many vital functions: it regulates body temperature, removes waste, helps to absorb nutrients and oxygen, cushions joints and so on. It's no wonder that we cannot survive long without it, and I'm grateful that a parched throat relentlessly reminds us when we need a top-up.

As God provided for the Hebrews physically, so he was also providing for them spiritually—just as he does today for anyone who will receive Jesus as Lord. Our spiritual lives cannot exist without the life-giving waters of Christ, but as we come to him, our spiritual rock, he will impart an unending, dependable supply of life-giving water by his Spirit.

That's why we need to come to our rock on a regular basis; otherwise our spiritual lives may dehydrate and consequently suffer.

Sitting next to a well in Samaria, Jesus said, 'All who drink this water will be thirsty again, but those who drink the water I give them will never thirst. Indeed, the water I give them will become in them a spring of water welling up to eternal life' (John 4:13–14).

We can try our best to be 'better' Christians, but unless we regularly come to Jesus and drink of his constant supply of living water, our 'Christian' endeavours will be a long, hard struggle of self-effort, draining our morale as well as our energy.

We can try to think up wise and helpful words to help other people, but unless we are being refreshed ourselves from the rock of living water, we will have nothing but human thought and opinions to offer—adequate to a point but barely comparable to the streams of living water that will flow out from lives whose source is Jesus.

Furthermore, unless we recognise our need of the rock, we are likely to look elsewhere for the inner satisfaction that our spirits crave. If we overlook the unwavering dependability of Jesus to supply our need of spiritual refreshment, health, cleansing and vitality, we may inadvertently seek to satisfy those spiritual needs through other sources.

But just as fizzy pop or caffeinated drinks can hardly compete with the sustenance we get from pure water, so nothing whatsoever can even begin to offer what we can only receive from our 'rock'.

A parched throat, lethargy, dry, pallid skin, muscle cramps and even hunger pangs can often be a sign that our body needs more water. But what about our spiritual life? Might that be thirsting for something more than it is receiving?

Are we feeling spiritually sluggish, insipid, uncomfortable or weak? Then let's come to Jesus, our rock—faithful, dependable, powerful and strong—and drink deeply of his living water.

'Let anyone who is thirsty come to me and drink. Whoever believes in me, as the Scripture has said, will have streams of living water flowing from within.' (John 7:37–38)

HOW TO QUENCH YOUR SPIRITUAL THIRST

Check your water supply

Our spiritual rock—Jesus—is our only source of spiritual refreshment, cleansing and empowering. Let's not be tempted to 'drink' only from Christian books about him, from testimonies about him, or even from other people's opinions about him. Rather, let's come to the rock for ourselves, recognising our spiritual thirst, and drink deeply of all that he wants to supply to rejuvenate our spiritual lives.

Read and reflect on John 4:13–14 and 7:37–39. Then consider the following.

- Do you recognise your spiritual thirst as keenly as you recognise your physical thirst?
- Do you crave that spiritual sustenance as much as you crave physical sustenance? 'Come, all you who are thirsty, come to the waters' (Isaiah 55:1).

My favourite herb is basil, so I always have a plant growing on my kitchen windowsill. Occasionally, I forget to water 'Basil' and within a day he begins to wilt: his leaves soften, then curl at the edges. After another day, his stem sags and eventually droops.

Provided I'm not too late, however, within a short time of replenishing his water supply, he transforms into what he was created to be. It's a stark reminder that Basil needs water every day.

The transforming power of water may not be so immediately obvious in our human body, let alone our spiritual lives, so let's keep Basil in mind when we neglect drinking from Jesus, our Rock. We need his spiritual water supply to transform us into his likeness and make us the person he created us to be. Let's not try to do it without him; otherwise we too will wilt and droop.

Don't give in to grumbling

Although God faithfully provided the Hebrews with water from a rock, he did not look favourably on their grumbling. In fact, they were punished. After all, grumbling against Moses and Aaron and complaining about desert life was, in fact, grumbling against God (Numbers 16:41–50).

The New Testament writers often admonish us to stop grumbling and complaining, because, as Paul reminds us, the Hebrews bore the consequences (1 Corinthians 10:10–11).

'Don't grumble against each other, brothers, or you will be judged' (James 5:9). 'Stop grumbling among yourselves' (John 6:43).

I have to admit that at times I fall prey to self-pity or am persuaded that my life would be better 'if only...' On such occasions, I have to take time to confess my grumbling and complaining and seek forgiveness for inadvertently dishonouring or misrepresenting God's love, purpose, provision and power through my self-centred, irrational or careless words of complaint.

I have to return to my spiritual rock and drink deeply of his spiritual life, which provides all that I need to quench the thirst of those inner cravings—to fulfil, equip and enrich me like nothing else this world could ever offer.

Do you ever grumble or complain—about your leaders, about the difficult aspects of your life, about unmet 'wants' or unfulfilled dreams? If so, then join with me and let's resolve to seek satisfaction from Jesus, our spiritual Rock. In so doing, may we all 'do everything without complaining or arguing, so that [we] may become blameless and pure, children of God without fault in a crooked and depraved generation, in which [we] shine like stars' (Philippians 2: 14–15).

Pray

O God, you are my God, earnestly I seek you; my soul thirsts for you, my body longs for you, in a dry and weary land where there is no water. I have seen you in the sanctuary and beheld your power and your glory. Because your love is better than life, my lips will glorify you. I will praise you as long as I live, and in your name I will lift up my hands. (Psalm 63:1–4)

Read

Exodus 17:1–7; Numbers 20:2–13; 1 Corinthians 10:1–13

JESUS:
RULER OF THE KINGS OF THE EARTH

Do you remember the General Election in 2010, when, for the first time, we watched three leading candidates debating live on television? Some voters found that helpful; others didn't, while a few admitted to being more interested in the colour of the candidates' ties than their fallible manifesto promises.

The question of whether or not we voted, and for whom, may have been influenced by a number of factors. Perhaps it was our perception of each candidate's moral integrity and their political party's stance on freedom for religious expression. We may have been swayed by the fact that one of the candidates professed to being a relatively active member of the Church of England, while another admitted that he had no faith. Perhaps we voted on the basis of their commitment to helping the poor, oppressed and marginalised, or their plans regarding refugees and asylum seekers. Or perhaps we based our choice on a strong personal conviction, without being able to explain the reason for our vote.

Whatever your feelings regarding the outcome of that particular election, please be encouraged, because God doesn't 'need' a Christian leader to fulfil his purposes. He is far more powerful than that. He made his Son, Jesus, 'the ruler of the kings of the earth', whether or not those 'kings' accept his rule (Revelation 1:5).

This emphatic scriptural statement makes it absolutely clear that Jesus has all authority over the 'kings'—leaders, rulers, presidents, prime ministers and tribal chieftains—of this world. His rule remains unhindered by the violence, corruption, injustice, oppression, greed and ungodliness we may at times witness among them.

The following conversation is recorded from Jesus' trial. '"Do you refuse to speak to me?" Pilate said. "Don't you realise I have power either to free you or to crucify you?" Jesus answered, 'You would have no power over me if it were not given to you from above"' (John 19:10–11).

Jesus' role as ruler of the kings of the earth is divinely empowered with the authority that God gave to him (Matthew 28:18)—the same authority that elevated Pontius Pilate to the position of Roman governor, overruled a pagan king's heart, brought an arrogant king to his knees and gave a prophetic word to the world through an unbelieving high priest. These are just a few examples to remind us that Jesus, who shares his Father's power, does indeed 'rule'.

CYRUS: THE PAGAN KING OF PERSIA

King Cyrus of Persia probably worshipped the god Ahura-mazda. Evidence, however, of his universal beliefs is expressed through the design, carvings and sculptures of his palatial buildings, which included influences of Baal, Ishtar, Apollo and Marduk. Furthermore, he assumed a policy of religious tolerance towards his subject peoples, even seeking ways to placate their gods where and when it suited his purposes.

God, however, overruled this man's heart in order to bring about his divine purpose. In fact, Cyrus was named in advance by the prophet Isaiah as the king whom God would use to restore his people from exile in Babylon, back to their promised land (Isaiah 44:28). And that's exactly what happened. Cyrus, perhaps with his eye on conquering Egypt, paid tribute to Yahweh and released the exiled Israelites, permitting them to return home and rebuild the temple in Jerusalem (Ezra 1:1–4).

Our leaders may appear to pay tribute to many people's belief systems, but Jesus will overrule their hearts in order to fulfil God's purpose.

NEBUCHADNEZZAR: THE ARROGANT KING OF BABYLON

Daniel reminded his captor, King Nebuchadnezzar, that it was God who had given him dominion over the nations (Daniel 2:36–38) and, after the episode in the lions' den, the king acknowledged that no one should speak against the Israelites' God (3:28–29).

Nevertheless, he remained proud; his token tribute was insufficient for God, who searches people's hearts. Later, Daniel interpreted a dream that foretold how God would humble the king. He reminded Nebuchadnezzar that 'the Most High is sovereign over the kingdoms on earth and gives them to anyone he wishes' (4:25), then urged him to renounce his sins so that his prosperity might continue (v. 27). But Nebuchadnezzar didn't do so.

In fact, just twelve months later, Nebuchadnezzar spoke those fateful words, 'Is not this the great Babylon I have built… by my mighty power and for the glory of my majesty?' (v. 30). Immediately, he was driven away; he ate grass like cattle and was drenched with dew. His hair grew like feathers and his nails like claws until he humbled himself before the true ruler of the earth and glorified the king of heaven (vv. 33–37).

Our leaders may appear to rule arrogantly, but 'those who walk in pride [God] is able to humble' (v. 37). In other words, 'Watch out!'

CAIAPHAS: THE UNBELIEVING HIGH PRIEST

Our religious leaders are not immune from our Lord's overruling power. The disciples believed in Jesus and must surely have longed that their religious leaders would, too, but the high priest Caiaphas refused to accept the evidence of Jesus' miraculous birth, his divine powers and fulfilment of messianic prophecy.

Despite his adherence to religious law, Caiaphas' heart was cold towards God, but God still used his prophetic role to proclaim that Jesus would be sacrificed for the nation(s)— words which have taught generations since to believe in that Passover sacrifice for their salvation from sin and spiritual death (John 11:49–52). Likewise, today's leaders may not be perfect but God can still use them to speak his word of truth.

Indeed, God has now given his authority to Jesus to be ruler of the kings of the earth, and he will overrule human plans and schemes as he determines. But he will not take his kingdom by force. Perfection will be restored only when he returns and consummates his kingdom at the end of the age. Consequently, today's leaders still have a choice whether or not to acknowledge Jesus as ruler, just as we do too.

The 'kings' of this world will be seen at times to lead with greedy, violent, oppressive, godless and sometimes faithless motives. But rest assured, there will come a day when every knee will bow and every tongue will admit that Jesus is Lord—that Jesus is the true and only ruler of the world (Philippians 2:10–11). Meanwhile, with such infallible hope for the future, Jesus gives us strength and encouragement to cope and witness for him today.

TAKE IT FURTHER

Pray for your leaders

I urge, then, first of all, that requests, prayers, intercession and thanksgiving be made for everyone—for kings and all those in authority, that we may live peaceful and quiet lives in all godliness and holiness. This is good, and pleases God our Saviour, who wants all people to be saved and to come to a knowledge of the truth. (1 Timothy 2:1–4)

Are we praying 'for' our leaders—or 'against' them? Ask Jesus to give you his perspective on their rule, his understanding of their hearts and his knowledge of the pressures or problems they face and the weight of responsibility they carry. Pray, too, for their salvation.

Believe in Jesus' overruling power

The Lord foils the plans of the nations; he thwarts the purposes of the peoples. But the plans of the Lord stand firm forever, the purposes of his heart through all generations. (Psalm 33:10–11)

Many are the plans in a human heart, but it is the Lord's purpose that prevails. (Proverbs 19:21)

Build up your faith with praise and thanksgiving that the Lord's purpose will prevail. Read and rejoice in Revelation 21. But, as you do so, continue to pray for your leaders and, as you feel led, write to them. In this way we are partners with God in the outworking of his divine purpose, in standing against spiritual forces of evil and, where necessary, speaking out on behalf of the poor, the oppressed and maltreated.

Be subject to rulers

Remind the people to be subject to rulers and authorities, to be obedient, to be ready to do whatever is good, to slander no one, to be peaceable and considerate, and to show true humility towards everyone. (Titus 3:1–2)

Believers are treated as second-class citizens and often persecuted in countries whose governments promote other religious faiths or atheism. Perhaps these leaders are worried that they will lose their faith-based influence over people who refuse to worship their gods; perhaps they are afraid that Christians will rebel against their laws. But that was never Jesus' teaching. He taught, 'Give to Caesar what is Caesar's, and to God what is God's' (Matthew 22:21).

Even in our own country, we are witnessing an increasing number of cases where Christians have been suspended or sacked from their jobs because they have acted on their Christian conscience, rather than abiding by what they perceive to be their employer's ungodly principles.

Jesus is Lord: to him we give our primary allegiance. As he is the ruler of the kings of the earth, so we all must seek his guidance for our own situation and respond accordingly. As we do so, let's keep Titus 3:1 in mind, along with our responsibility to love our enemy and bear witness through our behaviour to God's love and grace, while always being prepared to give a sound, scriptural answer 'with gentleness and respect' to those who ask us why we believe what we do (1 Peter 3:15).

JESUS:
THE TEACHER

I can recall many of my schoolteachers, but those who stand out in my memory are the few who really inspired me and those who were surly and strict. Parents, music tutors, church leaders and a few other memorable individuals have also 'mentored' different stages of my life's journey. But scripture reminds us that we have one true teacher, and that is Jesus Christ (Matthew 23:10).

In the comparatively short time that Jesus was ministering in Israel, others recognised and hailed him as Teacher (or Rabbi, which means the same thing: John 1:38). Some, however, were wary of his proclamations. After all, having been brought up in a poor carpenter's home, he had no recognised formal training. He hadn't spent years at the feet of an esteemed Jewish rabbi, learning the art of interpreting the law; nor had he even been trained as a scribe.

And yet, 'when the Sabbath came, he began to teach in the synagogue, and many who heard him were amazed. "Where did this man get these things?" they asked. "What's this wisdom that has been given him, that he even does miracles! Isn't this the carpenter? Isn't this Mary's son…?" And they took offence at him' (Mark 6:2–3). 'The Jews were amazed and asked, "How did this man get such learning without having studied?"' (John 7:15).

His accusers, who themselves swelled with pride when hailed as 'rabbi', denounced his supposedly impertinent assumption that one could feign the role of teacher on the basis of being self-taught. But Jesus continued to accept the title that others used for him and, in time, proclaimed himself the only Teacher. Whereas his contemporaries taught from the traditions and wisdom passed on to them from other men, Jesus declared, 'My teaching is not my own. It comes from him who sent me' (John 7:16).

That's why the crowds were also amazed—'because he taught as one who had authority, and not as their teachers of the law' (Matthew 7:29). Jesus' whole life, including his teaching, reflected the glory of the one who had sent him. The crowds recognised and applauded it, whether or not they actually comprehended it. But his fellow teachers regarded him with suspicion—jealous, perhaps, of his learning and acumen, afraid of losing their honourable status, offended by what they regarded as blasphemy.

Needless to say, their attempts to silence him didn't put Jesus off as he continued to obey his Father and make his kingdom known, both with words and in action. 'Jesus went through all the towns and villages, teaching in their synagogues, preaching the good news of the kingdom and healing every disease and sickness' (Matthew 9:35).

The nature and coming of the kingdom of God were fundamental to Christ's teaching ministry. Using many parables, he taught what the kingdom is like: a field sown with seed in which the enemy plants weeds, the positive permeating influence of yeast, the immense joy of finding precious treasure, the cancellation of gargantuan debts, the fruitfulness born of planting in good soil.

Jesus taught that God's kingdom resides in people rather than a place (Luke 17:21), in those who have surrendered to God's presence and purpose. Furthermore, he taught that those who humbly trust God and seek to live life his way, despite oppression, deprivation and even persecution, will experience the power and blessings of his kingdom both in this world and for ever (Matthew 5:3–10).

He instructed his disciples to pray for the kingdom to expand through the lives of submitted hearts (Matthew 6:10) and explained that those who accepted his teaching would live life to the full (John 10:10).

He expounded scripture, revealing himself as the long-promised Messiah (Matthew 5:17–18; 26:63–64), teaching that he was the only way to the Father (John 14:6). In turn, at the chosen time, he admitted to being God's kingly representative with authority to grant or hold back kingdom life, depending on whether a person acknowledged him as Lord (John 18:36–37; Revelation 3:7–8).

I could go on. Jesus didn't just teach in words, however, but also in action. Unlike his contemporaries, whom he slated for their hypocrisy, Jesus didn't teach one thing and then live by another; he lived up to his words (Matthew 23:13–31).

He didn't just tell the people about God's compassion, mercy, holiness, power and authority, but he also revealed and consequently taught those truths through his own life, as he touched lepers, forgave the adulteress, cleared the temple court, cast out demons, healed the sick and calmed the storm.

The source of Jesus' teaching was from God, and his lifestyle and actions lived up to his message, so revealing the nature and power of God through what he did.

But Jesus wasn't merely interested in people hearing and seeing his teaching; he longed for them to put it into practice. 'Anyone who chooses to do the will of God will find out whether my teaching comes from God or whether I speak on my own' (John 7:17). He recognised that people need to take a step of faith. If they took that step, his teaching would be reaffirmed as they saw its truths becoming reality in and through their lives.

Today, as in the first century AD, many people hear and see his teaching, but not everyone accepts it. Even when we do believe it, we may not always apply it consistently to our lives. Furthermore, we may be swayed by the wisdom and teaching of human beings, instead of being grounded in scripture.

So, if necessary, let's renew our respect for 'the Teacher' and, if we believe that what he says is true, let's be sure to put it into practice.

✳

LESSONS FROM OUR TEACHER

During his teacher training, my husband was taught the basic principle of how people learn: 'If you hear, you'll forget; if you see, you'll remember; if you do, you'll understand.'

I've certainly read about forgiveness, generosity, compassion, love, trust and so on, but I admit I can quickly forget them in the heat of the moment or the routine of life. Perhaps we can all recall people who've inspired us, individuals we've admired and remembered for the way they've put God's teaching into practice. But it's not until we put his teaching into practice ourselves that we'll understand its importance and learn to trust God in increasing measure.

So here are some lessons and homework from our Teacher, Jesus:

Subject: love

'Love one another. As I have loved you, so you must love one another' (John 13:34). For a definition of how to love, read 1 Corinthians 13:4–8. Is this how you love everyone you meet, no matter who they are, what they do or say or what they believe?

Subject: worry

'I tell you, do not worry about your life, what you will eat or drink; or about your body, what you will wear' (Matthew 6:25). Jesus taught that God knows what we need and will provide it (vv. 26–34). We may believe his teaching with our mind and yet harbour ongoing worries. If so, take time to accept and receive this truth to your heart—that God has promised to provide what you need for the life to which he has called you.

Subject: compassion in action

Read the parable of the good Samaritan (Luke 10:25–37). Jesus concludes by saying, 'Go and do likewise.' In what ways are you obeying his instruction?

Subject: materialism

'Watch out! Be on your guard against all kinds of greed; life does not consist in the abundance of possessions' (Luke 12:15). The words 'Watch out' and 'be on your guard' reveal how subtle our greed can be. What kind of 'wants' could be surreptitiously driving your heart and the use of your purse: new clothes every season, additional home accessories, a new car even when the current one works fine, the replacement of more than adequate furniture, the latest but unnecessary technology?

Subject: dedication

'Anyone who loves father or mother more than me is not worthy of me; anyone who loves son or daughter more than me is not worthy of me; those who do not take up their cross and follow me are not worthy of me' (Matthew 10:37–38). Does this teaching bear out in your life—in a wholehearted, unreserved commitment to the Lord?

Subject: trust

'Have faith in God' (Mark 11:22). 'Come' (Matthew 14:29). If Peter had clung on to the boat while testing whether the water would hold his weight, he would never have let go. It's only as we abandon our own ability, and trust in God to enable us to do what he asks, that we can appreciate the fullness of his promises. Do you need to let go? If so, remember to walk confidently in what he has asked you to do and not give in to your doubts (vv. 30–31).

Subject: forgiveness

'For if you forgive others when they sin against you, your heavenly Father will also forgive you. But if you do not forgive others their sins, your Father will not forgive your sins' (Matthew 6:14–15). You may need others to stand with you in prayer through the process of letting go of your hurt, but we all need to ensure we've responded to this clear, challenging teaching.

JESUS:
THE TRUE VINE

UNDERSTANDING THE IMAGE

After they had shared the Passover feast, Jesus led his disciples out of Jerusalem and up the Mount of Olives to Gethsemane. 'I am the true vine,' he told them (John 15:1). He spoke into the darkness, using a familiar term that once described God's people. They were planted in his promised land as a people who might know and love him, honour and serve him. Sadly, they were often admonished for diluting their reverence for God (Jeremiah 2:21), but, in Christ, the image of the vine was at last made complete. What Israel had failed to become, Christ fulfilled perfectly and, in so doing, promised spiritual sustenance to anyone who asked to be grafted into his life.

Jesus continues, 'I am the vine; you are the branches' (John 15:5a). It's only as we admit our need of Jesus' sacrifice on the cross that we can be reconciled to God. It's only as we accept Jesus as the provider of spiritual life that he breathes life into our being, grafting our spiritual lives into his eternal, resurrected life. And so we become the vine's branches.

Branches have a purpose beyond receiving life-giving sustenance, and that is to bear fruit. 'If you remain in me and I in you, you will bear much fruit; apart from me you can do nothing' (John 15:5b). Believers who truly depend on Christ will bear the fruit of the life-sustaining vine to which they are connected—and, in time, much fruit as they seek to 'remain' in him (vv. 2, 5, 8).

THE PROMISE

Most of us who long to know God more deeply, who desire to serve him well and leave his imprint on the world in which we live, surely relish the promises of John 15:1–17: that we will bear fruit (v. 5), that our prayers will be answered in the way we have asked (v. 7), that we shall experience joy (v. 11) and that we shall love others in the same phenomenal way that Jesus does (v. 12).

Some of us, however, might not feel as if these promises are being fulfilled in our lives, which is probably why Jesus kept re-emphasising his point: 'Remain in me, and I will remain in you. No branch can bear fruit by itself; it must remain in the vine. Neither can you bear fruit unless you remain in me' (v. 4).

Remaining in Jesus is complementary to having him remaining in us. As we take up and respond to his commands made available to us in scripture, Christ, who is the Word (John 1:1–2), remains in us. And so, as we maintain that union with the vine, Christ will in turn bear his fruit upon its branches—lives that display the evidence of his commands permeating our being.

As we 'remain' in the dimension of this spiritual union,

it affects the way we pray. Where once our prayers arose from our own thoughts and desires, the unhindered flow of Christ's life within overrides our own feelings and perceptions and overrules what we ask for in prayer. Rather than seeking that 'our' will be done, we genuinely seek that 'God's' will be done, and, when we pray Christ's prayers in perfect harmony with the will of God, they will inevitably be answered (John 15:7b–8). So, where once we may have experienced disillusionment from unanswered prayer, we shall instead experience Christ's joy in seeing the fruit of God's power at work in response to our requests.

Remaining in the vine also affects the way we relate to others. Christ loves all people equally, constantly and perfectly. Our natural tendency is to favour those to whom we easily relate, who are kind to us, towards whom we easily feel love and so on. Jesus, however, loved his closest friends as much as he loved his betrayer, his accusers and the mocking centurions who whipped him, punched him, tore out his hair and nailed him to the cross. That is only possible as the Spirit of God's perfect love for humanity flows through our lives, because God sees individuals from a different perspective: he wants to save them from Satan's dominion of spiritual death.

God has a plan and purpose for their lives and longs that they would know him as Father. As we remain in Christ, the Vine, that same love will flow through our hearts, too.

PUTTING IT INTO PRACTICE

To 'remain' in the vine, therefore, is an appealing image of intimacy with Jesus, stillness of soul, fruitfulness, answered prayer, joy and the capacity genuinely to love all people. Wouldn't that be great? But some of us may admit that much, if not most, of the product of our lives results from self-effort and natural ability, while others might say that their prayer life feels weak and ineffective or that they're simply finding it impossible to love a nasty neighbour.

So how do we 'remain' in the vine as Jesus intimated here?

By obeying his commands (v. 10)

Jesus is not implying here that one act of disobedience will nullify our salvation. If we want to bear fruit, however, we need to keep our connection to the vine free of any clutter that may hinder the flow of his Spirit, just as Jesus did by continually obeying his Father. Obedience is simply a choice: choosing to do what Jesus has asked us to do.

By spending time regularly alone in prayer

This is vital if we are to deepen our personal relationship with God, to hear his voice—receiving his comfort, guidance and discipline—to talk to him, worship him and relate to him on a spiritual dimension. In turn, this will strengthen and equip our spiritual life, maintaining a good connection to the vine.

By continuing to listen

Jesus isn't suggesting that we shut ourselves away in a prayer closet for the rest of our days. The whole point of bearing spiritual fruit is for Jesus to continue blessing others as he did when he lived in Israel. To 'remain' in him actually implies that we stay in that place where we depend on the flow of the spiritual life of Christ, resting in that spiritual union and communing with him in prayer, no matter what we're doing in our physical life.

So when we finish our time of personal prayer and set off for work or drop the children to school, when we get out the ironing board or chair a meeting, when we take our elderly neighbour to the shops or prepare to lead a Bible study, let's keep listening to the whispers of the Spirit to our conscience.

After all, only the Holy Spirit can bear the fruit of the Spirit, so we need to be attuned to his ways. When we feel tempted to do things our way, let's choose to obey his; when we feel convicted that we've let him down, let's restore that sweet connection through heartfelt confession. Ongoing prayer and obedience cannot fail to draw the vine's spiritual sustenance in and through our lives, resulting in the fruit that Christ intended.

By meditating on scripture

Keep in mind any words of scripture that he lays on your heart. Don't leave it back in the Sunday service or prayer closet: take it out into the day. Think about it; live by it; meditate on it. It may only be one short phrase or verse at a time, but as we put it into practice it will bear the fruit of a Christ-like, Christ-empowered life and the joy of answered prayer.

Believe me, letting his word remain in the forefront of the mind and heart will challenge speech, behaviour, attitude and activity—but it will also help us love others, as we choose to love them, no matter how we are feeling.

So let's remember, to 'remain' in the vine is to feel spiritually at home with Christ, no matter where we are or what we're doing. We'd never expect to see a branch jump off a vine, then trot around the garden trying to do its own thing. Branches stay put—constantly connected to their life-source. In fact, that's the only thing they do have to do; the rest is up to the flow of life that bears its fruit-giving properties.

TAKE IT FURTHER

Reflect

The garden of our church manse boasts two apple trees and a pear tree, plus our neighbour's grapevine weaving its way through the fence. I don't have to remember which tree is which, because each year I see apples, pears and even a few grapes hanging from their branches. The branch has no choice as to what kind of fruit it will bear; the fruit is the natural consequence of being attached to its respective vine or tree. Whose fruit are you bearing?

Pray

Lord, I realise that no matter how successful or admired my efforts may appear to be, spiritual fruit depends entirely on your life flowing through my activities. Holy Spirit, please keep this truth at the forefront of my conscience, so that I may always seek to glorify my Father. Amen

Read

John 15:1–17

JESUS:
THE TRUTH

UNDERSTANDING THE IMAGE

'Truth' is defined as something that can be proved to be real, either through knowledge or experience. So, for example, to prove what 'truth' is through knowledge, we use mathematical formulae, linguistic skills or scientific reasoning. To confirm what 'truth' is through experience, we make use of our five physical senses: sight, sound, touch, taste and smell.

Such learned or acquired truth, however, can never be absolute because further learning or experience over years (even centuries) may modify or even completely change what we had previously accepted as truth. Moreover, when we gauge 'truth' by these methods alone, we are limited to the parameters of human understanding and life in this physical world.

That's why, when Pilate asked Jesus, 'What is truth?' he didn't get an answer to his question, despite the fact that the answer was standing right in front of him (John 18:38). Jesus had just told Pilate that his purpose in being born was to testify to the truth (v. 37), but Jesus was speaking about the absolute, unchanging, fundamental truth concerning God's kingdom—something of which Pilate had no comprehension, as his knowledge and experience were limited to earthly kingdoms, political justice, physical power and human life.

'I AM... THE TRUTH'

Jesus said, 'I am the way and the truth and the life. No one comes to the Father except through me' (John 14:6). Jesus was born to testify to the truth about God because he was God. That which had always been outside the parameters of human understanding and experience was made flesh and brought within the reach of human beings.

Jesus not only taught about God as any religious leader would; Jesus provided the experience of God to human life. He embodied absolute truth—the reality of the complete knowledge and unadulterated experience of the divine, who created, sustains and rules this tangible world, to say nothing of the spiritual realm.

Sadly, like Pilate, many choose to reject absolute truth as revealed in the person of Christ and scriptural testimony, preferring to base life on relative truth, which changes according to culture, generation, authoritative persuasion, political correctness, perceived human rights and the ongoing advancement of knowledge. In fact, many people slate the perceived arrogance of Christian belief, which declares that it has the absolute truth in preference to any other religion.

But Jesus wasn't arrogant in his declaration. He stated it simply as fact: as God incarnate, he represented the divine being, character, nature, purpose, word and works of God.

'I TELL YOU THE TRUTH'

Matthew, Mark, Luke and John all quote many instances when Jesus said, 'I tell you the truth…', a choice phrase re-affirming that his words were not just his own but originated with God (John 12:49–50). Like Jesus, we will find that our 'telling of the truth' will be received and understood differently, depending on whom we are speaking to.

To the unbeliever…

For many of them, the 'truth' of what is real and right depends on human knowledge, understanding and opinion—the capacity for the human brain to understand the physical world and experience it via electrical impulses received from the five sense receptors (sight, hearing, touch, taste and smell). To try to argue or debate absolute truth with someone who rejects the idea of spiritual life as naïve superstition is futile.

We should continue to pray for the opening of their spiritual eyes and remain willing to respond to their questions, but let's not exhaust ourselves in endless dead-end argument with the spiritually uninitiated. After all, Jesus didn't waste his strength trying to defend himself with Pilate: his main concern was to reveal truth to Pilate's pagan heart, and sometimes this is achieved more effectively through actions than words and through the spiritual outworking of God's power and purpose.

So, 'in your hearts set apart Christ as Lord. Always be

prepared to give an answer to everyone who asks you to give the reason for the hope that you have. But do this with gentleness and respect' (1 Peter 3:15). 'Don't have anything to do with foolish and stupid arguments, because you know they produce quarrels' (2 Timothy 2:23). 'The god of this age has blinded the minds of unbelievers, so that they cannot see the light of the Gospel of the glory of Christ, who is the image of God... Though we live in the world, we do not wage war as the world does. The weapons we fight with are not the weapons of the world. On the contrary, they have divine power to demolish strongholds. We demolish arguments and every pretension that sets itself up against the knowledge of God' (2 Corinthians 4:4; 10:3–5).

To the interested enquirer...

They are sympathetic to spiritual truth, but unanswered questions prevent them from accepting Christ and submitting to him as Lord. Such questions tend to arise from a quest for philosophical truth: for example, why, if God is loving, does he allow suffering in the world and why would he send a perceived 'good' person to hell?

Jesus said, 'If you hold to my teaching... you will know the truth, and the truth will set you free' (John 8:31–32). Knowing this truth doesn't imply that we shall understand everything there is to know about God's ways and God's will: if that were the case, we would be God ourselves! God, his ways and his thoughts, being in very nature self-existent, eternal and divine, can never be comprehended by created mortals. Rather, when Jesus said this, he spoke of freedom from the consequences of sin.

Jesus won't provide every answer to the questions we have concerning this life or its difficulties, and he doesn't offer a formula to set wrong things right; instead, he offers himself. It's only in a trusting relationship with him that absolute truth imparts God's peace, security, fulfilment and hope, dovetailing the eternal spiritual life with the temporary physical life.

To the Christian...

Here is someone who seeks to uphold absolute truth in a world that rejects, mocks and increasingly persecutes the declaration of that truth. As if that's not hard enough, even within our own circles we debate the truth about women in leadership, infant baptism, drinking alcohol, the wearing of hats in church, and so on.

'The law was given through Moses; grace and truth came through Jesus Christ', who said, 'I will ask the Father, and he will give you another Counsellor to be with you for ever—the Spirit of truth. The world cannot accept him, because it neither sees him nor knows him. But you know him, for he lives with you and will be in you… But when he, the Spirit of truth, comes, he will guide you into all truth. He will not speak on his own; he will speak only what he hears, and he will tell you what is yet to come' (John 1:17; 14:16–17; 16:13).

God's truth was only ever fully revealed in and through Christ. The law that he gave through Moses wasn't wrong, but it was incomplete. In Jesus, however, absolute truth has been unveiled so that anyone can know and experience the reality of God through the Holy Spirit.

Paul said, 'Since we live by the Spirit, let us keep in step with the Spirit' (Galatians 5:25). If we want to know and walk in truth, we must depend on Jesus to guide us and then obey what he commands. Our aim is not to know the truth about every subject, but to know the truth about God—his holy ways and sovereign purposes—as revealed in Christ, and now to our hearts by the Holy Spirit. Nor do we seek to obey a set of laws, whose divine and therefore higher ways we may or may not think we understand; rather, we seek to live according to the love of God as revealed and given out to us in Christ. And we do so through the Holy Spirit.

Unless we submit to the Spirit's promptings, we have no reliable guide to accompany and direct us through the ups and downs, the perplexities and unanswered questions of life. But when we keep in step with his ways, we learn to live by God's absolute truth. Furthermore, 'whoever lives by the truth comes into the light, so that it may be seen plainly that what he has done has been done through God' (John 3:21).

Surely there is no better incentive to walk in truth—in step with Jesus by the Holy Spirit—than to live lives that are pleasing to the Lord, knowing that, as we do so, others will experience God for themselves.

TAKE IT FURTHER

Reflect

Only Jesus could say, 'I am the truth' and live up to the morals implied by his declaration. Nevertheless, if we claim to know the truth, we must then allow that truth to have absolute authority as we seek to live according to the ways of the one who lives within.

Pray

Father, there are times when I try to fathom the unfathomable. Grant me wisdom to know what to study, understand, learn and obey, and what will always remain far higher than my thoughts and far higher than my ways (Isaiah 55:9).

Read

John 18:28–40; 2 Corinthians 3:3–6

JESUS:
THE WAY

I used to take pride in my map-reading skills, even if occasionally I did turn the map upside down to clarify left and right. So I felt a bit put out when my husband changed his allegiance to a satnav, the marvellous piece of technological gadgetry that promises to show you the way to wherever you want to go.

I must admit, it's been an absolute gem when trying to navigate alone through busy traffic in unfamiliar town centres. Nevertheless, it makes mistakes, too—and many of us may have heard of cars being rescued from rivers, lorries getting stuck under bridges and drivers being taken hundreds of miles off route, owing to satnav errors.

Fortunately, the way to God does not appear on a map or a set of directions, let alone a dodgy satnav. Rather, the way to God is a person.

John 14 opens with Jesus gently trying to encourage his disciples, urging them not to be afraid about his impending departure, painting for them a beautiful picture of where he was going and why he had to go, promising he would return, and reminding them that they already knew how to get there. But, discouraged, bewildered and shot through with anticipatory dread, Thomas responds as if he's barely been listening: 'Lord, we don't know where you are going, so how can we know the way?'

How can we know the way? It is such an important question—the way to an eternal life in heaven and the way to experiencing the fullness of God in the lives that we live today, no matter what our situation.

Jesus answered, 'I am the way and the truth and the life. No one comes to the Father except through me' (v. 6). In one short verse, Jesus succinctly conveys a truth of unprecedented significance. In our search for the way to eternal life and the way to making life meaningful now, there is only one path—and that is himself.

THE WAY TO GOD: FOR ETERNITY

Up until that point, generations had been restricted to an impersonal knowledge of God. They witnessed the Spirit's anointing on certain chosen men and women to prophesy, teach and guide, and relied on the tribe of Levi (the men who had been set apart as priests) to approach God's presence on their behalf in the sanctuary of his holy temple.

But Jesus came to provide a way for all people to meet with God personally. At the very moment he gave up his spirit on the cross, offering to God his perfect life as the sacrifice for all our faults, failings and misdemeanours—past, present and future—the heavy curtain in the temple that separated the people from the holiest place of God's presence was torn in two from top to bottom. The way had been reopened for fallen humankind to approach God, to be reconciled with him and to enjoy the personal, intimate relationship that he had always envisaged for his beloved people.

Jesus didn't say he is 'a way', rather that he is 'the only way' to the Father. And I, along with many others, have been accused of intolerance and condemned as a dogmatic bigot for believing and promoting this belief.

Nevertheless, no matter what may be hurled at us, it cannot be disputed that Jesus is the only man who ever declared that he was God's Son, who proved it through his works and words (14:11) and qualified his claim to be the only way to God through his unique resurrection from the dead. No one else could even try to claim that.

'Salvation is found in no one else, for there is no other name under heaven given to people by which we must be saved' (Acts 4:12). 'For there is one God and one mediator between God and human beings, Christ Jesus, himself human, who gave himself as a ransom for all' (1 Timothy 2:5–6).

Consequently, no other religious leader, subsequent to their death, has ever been able to accompany, equip and encourage their disciples as the living Lord Jesus continues to do through the Holy Spirit. Indeed, we don't have to wait until we get to heaven to know God. Jesus is the way to experience him today.

THE WAY TO GOD: FOR THE PRESENT

Jesus was, is and will always be intimately connected with his Father. Having confirmed that he was the way to eternal life in God's presence (John 14:1–6), Jesus continued, 'If you really knew me, you would know my Father as well… Anyone who has seen me has seen the Father… Don't you believe that I am in the Father, and that the Father is in me? The words I say to you are not just my own. Rather, it is the Father, living in me, who is doing his work' (vv. 7, 9–10).

Jesus simply reiterated what he'd proclaimed throughout his ministry—that everything he said, did and revealed originated in God's purpose and character.

As God's purpose and character are the only worthy goals in this life, then we need to accept Jesus as the only way to experiencing those things—the way to experiencing peace, fulfilment, self-worth, provision, contentment, security, protection, guidance and so many other qualities and assurances in life.

The way that Jesus offers isn't merely a path to the final goal of our journey: as Jesus is the embodiment of God's truth and life, he brings that destination within our reach today. And so, by believing in Jesus as the way to God, we have in this life our assurance of eternity in his perfect presence—the place that Jesus said he was going to prepare for us (v. 2). For the time being, however, as we hold on to our hope that Jesus will return one day as promised and take us there (v. 3), we may appreciate and engage with that life by remaining on the way to it—by keeping close to Jesus—rather than being led astray by alternative 'ways' to an alternative life that the world will constantly offer.

TAKE IT FURTHER

If you have time, read John 14:1–31.

Are you like Philip?

'Don't you know me, Philip, even after I have been among you such a long time?' (John 14:9)

When Philip first met Jesus, he responded to Christ's discipleship call without hesitation, believing him to be the Messiah and setting off immediately to win another convert (John 1:43–46). Three years passed, during which time, living in close proximity to Jesus, Philip observed and experienced his unconditional love, powerful miracles and profound wisdom on a daily basis. And yet, at the end of that time, it seems that he still failed entirely to recognise God's handprint upon it (14:8).

Thankfully, Philip pulled through. He later met the resurrected Jesus, joined with the disciples in prayer and, according to history, died a martyr. But what about you?

- Do you feel as if you've lost your way in life?
- Has your perspective been eroded over time? Have you been bogged down by theological debate, persecution, relentless difficulties, busyness, compromise, apathy or simply spending too much time away from Jesus?

Isaiah promised, 'A bruised reed he will not break, and a smouldering wick he will not snuff out' (Isaiah 42:3). Draw near to Jesus—the way to God—and he will draw near to you (James 4:8).

Are you like Thomas?

'How can we know the way?' (v. 5)

Jesus answered, 'I am the way and the truth and the life… I will ask the Father, and he will give you another Counsellor to be with you forever—the Spirit of truth… I will not leave you as orphans.' (vv. 5–6, 16–18)

It was nigh on impossible for Thomas and, in fact, all the disciples to comprehend what Jesus was saying. They were bewildered, afraid and upset. When Jesus was arrested and crucified, they fled and hid themselves away.

But Jesus—the 'way' to God's peace, strength, security, provision, equipping, wisdom, guidance, power, discernment, purpose, acceptance and love—returned and lived within them by his Spirit.

Have we, too, known Jesus for years and enjoyed his company when life was smooth, but panicked when trouble hit hard? Do we allow irrational, illogical thoughts to overrule our mind and hearts and deafen us to Jesus' voice?

• Which way do you turn when you want to find peace? Mundane TV, alcohol, a relentless pursuit of your side of the argument—or Jesus?

- Which way do you turn when you want to find comfort? Shopping, someone else's arms, unnecessary food—or Jesus?
- Which way do you turn when you want to find strength? Self-help books, fanatical fitness régimes, emotional defence mechanisms—or Jesus?
- Which way do you turn when you want to find guidance? Other people's opinions, decisions or expectations of you, your own plans and schemes—or Jesus?
- Which way do you turn when you want to find purpose? Your own aspirations, cultural expectations and temptations—or Jesus?
- Which way do you turn when you want to find self-worth? A slimmer figure, new clothes, a partner, parenthood, your career—or Jesus?
- Which way do you turn when you want to find fulfilment? Longer working hours, a job that pays more money, an overfull diary of activities, social engagements and responsibilities—or Jesus?

Pray

Jesus, I am reminded that you are the only way to God, the only way to eternal life, the only way to a fulfilled, contented, meaningful life today. Please help me to remain on your way when I am tempted to take other paths. Amen

JESUS:
THE WISDOM OF GOD

I admire Christians who can confidently debate Christianity with today's unbelieving orators, skilled in the art of communicating atheist and humanist convictions. Indeed, I am grateful for my brothers and sisters in Christ who've accepted invitations to debate publicly the faith that I hold to so dearly, but which I can't explain as eloquently or convincingly.

Unlike some, I get rather tongue-tied when my faith is shot down by scientific expertise or humanist philosophy, as I'm not always able to dispute alleged 'fact' with an acceptably intelligent response. Nevertheless, human knowledge, intelligence and argumentative skill, which may sometimes be used to counter intellectual unbelief, are quite different from the wisdom of God, which is available to us all.

UNDERSTANDING THE IMAGE

God is the source of all wisdom (Job 12:13; Psalm 51:6; Proverbs 2:6), and so Jesus, being the essence of his Father's nature, expressed God's love, justice, righteousness and wisdom to the world.

In fact, Jesus began to show its signs from a tender age —a profound wisdom that continued to amaze his contemporaries throughout adulthood (Luke 2:40, 52; Matthew 13:54). But it wasn't seen only in his acute perceptions of life and faith; the whole purpose of his coming and dying encompassed the plan that God devised, in his wisdom, to provide forgiveness and reconciliation through the cross of Christ. And this wasn't any easier for first-century Palestine to grasp than it is for the 21st-century Western world.

When Paul wrote to the Corinthian church, crucifixion was still considered a fitting punishment for the lowest of criminals—not what one would expect for enlightened men of moral standing and definitely not for one deemed worthy of worship.

'But God chose the foolish things of the world to shame the wise; God chose the weak things of the world to shame the strong' (1 Corinthians 1:27). He did this in order that we might never think we could gain salvation through intellectual ability, skilful competence, persuasive proclamations, moralistic ideals or outward pious behaviour—only through believing in the cross of Christ, no matter how foolish that might appear.

CHRIST, THE WISDOM OF GOD: AT THE HEART OF OUR FAITH

Paul's Jewish contemporaries expected a Messiah, but misjudged his coming in their quest for a sign of majestic power and political prowess. To uphold Christ's crucifixion as a means to salvation was utterly offensive to them.

Meanwhile, the Greek philosophers were so absorbed in intellectual speculation that few had time for the gospel message. To entertain the idea that God would use crucifixion as the means to forgive sins was dismissed as sheer folly.

It's not so very different today. Crucifixion may not feature so heavily in our generation but, as Christians, we too are scorned for accepting this barbaric act at the core of our faith in a loving God, out of which we trust in the resurrected Lord Jesus Christ.

Indeed, such thinking is deemed sheer madness by many esteemed as the 'wise' of this world. I've heard the gospel mocked and denounced in a variety of ways, as a far-fetched fairytale or the brutal fantasy of a masochistic deity. But just who are the 'wise man, scholar and philosopher' of this present but passing age (1 Corinthians 1:20)?

Perhaps they are perceived to be the intellectual or scientifically acclaimed orators who only believe in what can be proved through their own devised formulae and scientific tests, or through what they perceive with their physical senses —sight, sound, touch, taste and smell. Sadly, however, this closes the door on the reality of a far more powerful, yet unseen, supernatural spiritual realm.

Perhaps they are today's academic philosophers—those who pursue truth through their own understanding of the cycle of life as seen in nature, observed from history or inspired by other thinkers. They are steeped in the concepts devised by the created, but lacking any reference to the ways of their creator.

Or perhaps the 'wise' of today are considered as those who give much of their time, energy and resources into doing 'good' things, those who appear to live a 'good' lifestyle, those devoted to religious ritual or renowned for their pious behaviour—exhibiting 'a form of godliness', but one that denies its power (2 Timothy 3:5).

Whoever the 'wise' may be, such 'wisdom' will pass with the age and only one will remain: the wisdom of God, as revealed in Jesus Christ. We do not receive salvation through being wise—whatever shape or form that wisdom should take—but through faith. Indeed, 'the message of the cross is foolishness to those who are perishing, but to us who are being saved it is the power of God' (1 Corinthians 1:18). The question to ask is: are we willing to be labelled a 'fool' for making it known that we believe?

Furthermore, the world esteems those who are financially successful; it admires those with intellectual or physical ability and defers to those with persuasive skills of leadership. Generally, much of the world laughs at those whose primary concern is knowing and submitting to Jesus, the wisdom of God, who is our righteousness, holiness and redemption (1 Corinthians 1:30).

So, what is our boast (vv. 29–31)? What is the source of our sense of self-worth? In whom or what do we really put our trust? Is it in the current trends of 'wisdom' that inspire respect from the world or the security of our relationship with Christ?

I have to admit that when I focus on the outward person who is sneering at my faith, belittling my understanding and rejecting me as a friend or relative, I'm gutted: in fact, the world's wisdom can even unsettle my sense of self-worth and confidence. But as I remain in Christ and his wisdom, he helps me to perceive the inner person who isn't just rejecting me, but is rejecting God, who yearns for their soul.

Even the great communicator Paul knew what he was up against when he preached the simplicity of the gospel to a supposedly wise and intellectual audience, but that didn't stop him talking. Although the world perceived his message as 'foolishness', he knew that it held power to save lives from spiritual death. So I am encouraged to persevere by keeping in mind God's heart for the lost and making Christ known, no matter how my message is received.

CHRIST, THE WISDOM OF GOD: OFFERING GUIDANCE FOR TODAY

Believing and trusting in Christ, the wisdom of God, isn't just important for witnessing; it's also fundamental to the rest of our lives. So we read, 'If any of you lacks wisdom, you should ask God, who gives generously to all without finding fault, and it will be given to you' (James 1:5).

Indeed, the supremacy of divine wisdom, deemed foolish in the world, is the means to guide our life's journey. Scripture promises that we will be given wisdom to speak when persecuted for our faith, to cope with difficulties, to preach and to understand and know God better, to name just a few examples.

We cannot accept the cross of Christ at the heart of our faith without allowing his wisdom to influence and pervade our everyday lives. There are all kinds of choices we make concerning how to use our time: which relationships to pursue, what standards of behaviour to adopt and what kind of lifestyle to live. For every choice, the wisdom of the world will be only too pleased to offer its opinion.

Some time ago, God clearly guided me to resign from a successful and financially rewarding career to pursue his chosen paths for my life, but someone very close to me called me a fool. Nevertheless, when God speaks he expects us to respond, no matter what others may say or how they may hurt us.

I'm certainly no saint and I have got it wrong at times—hastily seeking out a worldly means of resolving a problem without first giving adequate time to prayer, to seek the Lord for his wisdom for resolving or managing the situation. I've learnt from my mistakes in the same way that I've learnt, while out on a walk, not to go off the path when the map clearly tells me to stay on it. Overgrown brambles, ankle-wrenching divots, wearisome dead ends and the unsettled anxiety that looms large when you're not sure where you're heading are much akin to the scratchy relationships, emotional hurts, fatigue, insecurity and lack of peace that arise from living life by worldly wisdom rather than the Lord's.

So, next time we need help, let's seek the Lord for wisdom and believe in his promise to give it—but when we ask, let's believe and not doubt (James 1:6), and trust in his perfect purpose, perfect time and perfect love in the outcome.

✳

TAKE IT FURTHER

Reflect

The fear of the Lord is the beginning of wisdom, and knowledge of the Holy One is understanding. (Proverbs 9:10)

There is no other way to gain true, eternal and unshakeable wisdom than by revering and seeking the Lord.

Pray

Oh Lord, I sometimes feel inadequate when the world puts me down for believing in you and for following in your ways. But thank you that you are indeed true wisdom—and in that knowledge I rest secure, no matter what others may throw at me as I share your heart for the lost.

Read

1 Corinthians 1:17—2:16; James 1:2–8

JESUS:
WONDERFUL COUNSELLOR

Each year, the media report the bestselling Christmas gifts and the top ten presents most wanted by children. But if I were to ask what you would most like for Christmas, I wonder how you would reply. What would be at the top of your list of wants?

Perhaps it would be a particular 'toy', accessory, gadget, addition to your wardrobe, CD, piece of jewellery, ambition fulfilled or mortgage repaid. Or perhaps it would be to enjoy the company of a relative or friend, to see your spouse or child safely returned from overseas army service, to be healed of a painful, worrying or long-term illness. Perhaps you would long to unwrap the promise of a new job, relationship or home.

So, if you are faced with anything but that which you long for, do turn with me to a real, tangible and promised gift that was given with the birth of Jesus: 'There will be no more gloom for those who were in distress… For to us a child is born, to us a son is given, and the government will be on his shoulders. And he will be called Wonderful Counsellor' (Isaiah 9:1, 6).

GOD'S GIFT

The government of God's kingdom has been handed to his Son, King Jesus. Kings require many attributes to qualify them to rule well—power, wisdom and authority, for example—but, by no means least, they need sound counsel.

A counsellor isn't just someone who gives advice or guidance; the word also describes a person who determines a plan and carries out a programme of action. That's exactly what Jesus did. He followed through with God's plan. He rescued his people from captivity to Satan's dominion, returning them to the realm of God's presence and eternal life.

So, the vulnerable baby born in a Bethlehem stable was central to God's purpose. For eternity he has been intimately acquainted with God's counsel, but, in coming to earth as a man, he was given a name, an identity that he personified perfectly: Wonderful Counsellor. Wonderful, as in divine, supernatural, exceptional, distinguished, and Counsellor, meaning the one who would put God's plan into action.

The baby Jesus would grow up to fulfil his monumental role by offering himself to die on our behalf and, in so doing, conquer Satan's hold over spiritual death. If we believe and accept him as our Lord, Jesus activates God's plan in our lives and releases us from the gloom and distress of living in a fallen world ravaged by Satan's evil antics; he releases us from a life and death exiled from God's presence.

GOD'S PROMISE

There may be aspects of our Christmas celebrations that stress, depress or excite us, but, if we will keep at the forefront of our mind the truth of Isaiah's prophecy, here is a gift to enthuse our lives every day and in every circumstance— not just on 25 December. Jesus continues, in his role as Wonderful Counsellor, to guide and equip us through life. And if we choose to follow and fulfil his wise advice and divine purpose, we shall each play our unique part in the outworking of God's plan in our generation, as well as in our Christmas preparations and celebrations.

'The Spirit of the Lord will rest on him—the Spirit of wisdom and of understanding, the Spirit of counsel and of power, the Spirit of knowledge and of the fear of the Lord' (Isaiah 11:2). Jesus fulfilled God's counsel, empowered by the Holy Spirit, and the same Spirit that rested on Jesus now rests on us. The Counsellor is ever present to guide us and equip us in fulfilling our unique potential in the outworking of God's purposes (John 14:15–18). But are we listening? Moreover, are we obeying?

OUR CHOICE

We can say we believe that God has a sovereign plan for this world and its redemption from evil; we can also admit that we believe he has a purpose for everyone to play within the overall outworking of his plan. But we have to listen to, follow and obey the directions of our Wonderful Counsellor if we want to put those beliefs into practice.

If we prefer our own way of doing things, our beliefs amount to nothing more than talk. Sadly, God's promise of a fulfilled life will continue to evade us, while the name 'Wonderful Counsellor' will merely be words on a page.

Circumstances in the world—life's setbacks, tragedies, heartaches, and even Christmas itself—can so easily distract us from his presence, let alone his empowering, but we each have a choice to make. Will we let this sin-filled world drag us down with it or will we choose the gift of Jesus who enables us to respond to this world with hope, purpose and the power of his Spirit?

This is the outstanding truth proclaimed with great gusto in Handel's oratorio *Messiah*, part of which sets Isaiah 9:6 to music: 'For unto us a child is born... and his name shall be called Wonderful Counsellor.' I've just set it playing via YouTube while writing this study. If you get a chance, do listen to it, and I trust that this study will spur you on to join in the refrain with equal gusto, inspired with renewed passion and thanksgiving for what Christ's name implies.

UNWRAP THE GIFTS

The gift of his presence

In him we were also chosen, having been predestined according to the plan of him who works out everything in conformity with the purpose of his will. (Ephesians 1:11)

God's counsel—his plan that has not changed down the ages (Isaiah 25:1; Psalm 33:11)—is to live in perfect union with his people, loving them, providing for them, empowering them, fulfilling them and being loved by them in return.

Satan's dominion always seeks to disrupt, deceive, dissuade, discourage and divert our attention and belief in God's purpose, but Jesus, our Wonderful Counsellor, provides the way for us to work out that plan in all circumstances.

Are we choosing to conform 'to the purpose of his will' in every area of our lives, seeking each day to actively 'work out our salvation' (Philippians 2:12)?

The gift of his purpose

For we are God's workmanship, created in Christ Jesus to do good works, which God prepared in advance for us to do. (Ephesians 2:10)

Do you feel that your life looks like a piece of modern art in the making—a splash of colour here, a scrawl of squiggles there, which leaves you guessing haphazardly what kind of picture God had in mind when he designed its random parts? If so, then ask Jesus, the Wonderful Counsellor, to refresh your heart with his perspective.

Our loving Father planned our lives from design stage to completion—lives filled with his ongoing potential and purpose to fulfil his will and satisfy our needs, physically, mentally, emotionally and spiritually.

Jesus said, 'I have come that they may have life, and have it to the full' (John 10:10), and that's his gift to you today—in fact, every day, if you choose to receive it and live it out.

The gift of his power

For it is God who works in you to will and to act according to his good purpose. (Philippians 2:13)

Paul was chosen as an apostle to the Gentiles but recognised that it was only by God's grace and empowering that he could fulfil this role—certainly not through any merit of his own. Consequently, engaging with life from God's perspective, he simply got on with the job in hand, despite opposition, difficult people, hardships, imprisonment, a human sense of inadequacy, and so on.

Are you willing to surrender to the wisdom, will and way of the Wonderful Counsellor so that you too can realise God's plan through your life?

The spiritual blessings

Praise be to the God and Father of our Lord Jesus Christ, who has blessed us in the heavenly realms with every spiritual blessing in Christ. (Ephesians 1:3)

The heavenly realm—the spiritual environment—where forces of good and evil continue to battle for control over our minds and hearts is the arena of spiritual blessing for those of us who are in Christ. These priceless gifts are available to every believer: an intimate relationship with God, spiritual power, comfort, purpose, boldness and strength, to name only a few mentioned in Paul's letters.

Our worldly wants can never compare to these permanent,

life-imbued, purpose-filled blessings, but it's only as we follow the Wonderful Counsellor and set our sights on this heavenly realm that we begin to appreciate their value and potential.

So again I ask, what do you most long for? I trust that any wants in this world will pale in the light of these promised gifts. The presence, guidance and equipping of the Wonderful Counsellor has your name on its gift-tag. Will you choose to receive, open and enrich your life with all that he has to offer?

Pray

God can do 'immeasurably more than all we ask or imagine, according to his power that is at work within us' (Ephesians 3:20).

I will praise the Lord, who counsels me; even at night my heart instructs me. I have set the Lord always before me. Because he is at my right hand, I shall not be shaken. (Psalm 16:7–8)

Read

Isaiah 9:1–7

JESUS:

THE WORD OF GOD

'Sticks and stones may break my bones, but words shall never hurt me.' Do you remember saying these words in the school playground when someone said something unkind? I do—and it was a response that emboldened me to hold my head high as I stomped off with my friends. But if I'm honest, deep inside, those unkind words did hurt terribly, and it wouldn't have taken much for my tears to invite another barrage of verbal abuse if I'd dissolved into a 'crybaby'.

Words are more than just sounds; they have dynamic power. If I speak unkindly to a person, my words may hurt and even damage their emotional, psychological or spiritual well-being. Furthermore, when Isaac unwittingly spoke his blessing over Jacob, Esau begged Isaac to bless him, too, but the words had already been spoken and could not be retracted (Genesis 27:1–40). Since this is true of human words, then how much more with God's?

God spoke and, by his words, the heavens and the earth came into being (Genesis 1); 'he sent forth his word and healed them' (Psalm 107:20); his word has power like a hammer that can break a rock into pieces (Jeremiah 23:29).

Indeed, when God sends out his word, it never returns to him empty but accomplishes his purpose (Isaiah 55:11). And so we read John's powerful introduction to his Gospel: 'In the beginning was the Word, and the Word was with God, and the Word was God' (1:1).

UNDERSTANDING THE IMAGE

The Word of God

Jesus did not come into being at the moment of his conception in Mary's womb, but has always been a person of the Godhead. Nevertheless, he has a distinct role from God the Father, here described as 'the Word'—the effective power that carries out God's command. All that was created was made by him, and everything that has life finds its life in him —physical, mental, emotional and spiritual (John 1:3–4).

But the name 'Word of God' implies more than the outworking of his command. Just as our speech expresses our thoughts, so the Word of God conveys and communicates who he is. The Word was with God before time began, but until the Word was clothed in the flesh of Jesus, the essence of God was only partially known through his created world, his intervention in individual lives and his messages relayed through prophets. No one had ever seen God, but Jesus— the Word made flesh—made him known (v. 18).

The Word became flesh

My husband sometimes describes me as a 'wordsmith' instead of a 'writer', as he knows how I enjoy teasing out different meanings of words, trying different combinations to see how they best fit together, then pruning and polishing them into a final creation. Perhaps that's why I enjoy playing games based on words, especially charades—trying to guess a word or phrase while somebody acts it out. But although it's just a game, charades also helps us to understand the Word made flesh.

In the same way that a participant displays the meaning of a word through her actions, so Jesus made God known through the visible expression of God's power, wisdom and character displayed through his life.

Every so often, someone says to me that if only God would reveal himself to them, then they would believe in him. But God has already done that fully in the person of Jesus Christ, who, as the Word of God, revealed his Father perfectly. 'He is the image of the invisible God… the radiance of God's glory and the exact representation of his being' (Colossians 1:15; Hebrews 1:3). He was the divine expressed in human form and, through faithful witness, his testimony is preserved in the writings of holy scripture, made alive to our hearts today by his eternal Spirit.

If we want to see the Word of God—if we want to see God's power, wisdom, purpose and character at work— we just need to look to Jesus and believe in who he is. The Word of God became flesh so that we may see God's power at work through miraculous physical healings, God's wisdom in the things that Jesus taught, God's righteousness in his dealings with religious and political leaders, God's forgiveness displayed to the woman caught in adultery and God's sovereignty in his authority over demons.

We can see the beauty of God's holiness in the way that Jesus lived his life, God's transcendent majesty in his transfigured body, and God's love in action as he washed his friends' feet before dying a cruel death on our behalf. Perhaps most crucially, we can know God's victory over Satan in the resurrection of Christ. Indeed, we have seen God's glory in his Word who became flesh, 'full of grace and truth' (John 1:14).

Bible studies, however, are not simply intended to expand our head knowledge; they are also a means to help us nurture our relationship and walk with God, to help us put what we've learnt into practice. So what does this understanding of the Word of God imply for us today?

PUTTING IT INTO PRACTICE

We are to continue his witness

Jesus was no mere charade, who only ever intended to create a good impression about God: Jesus was (and is) God. When we believe in and accept Jesus as our Lord, the Spirit of God comes to live within our lives (Ephesians 1:13–14), guaranteeing our inheritance in heaven and providing the means for the Word of God to continue his tangible witness in the world.

Paul criticised certain people who had a form of godliness but denied its power (2 Timothy 3:5), whose charade of faith was a mere pretence of piety, because we are called to be Christ's ambassadors so that God can continue to make his appeal through us (2 Corinthians 5:20). In the same way that the Word revealed God to the world, so we have a responsibility to continue his visible witness.

We are to love one another

As Francis of Assisi said, 'Go out and preach the gospel, and if you have to, use words.' The Bible provides plenty of instruction as to how we can do this, so let's take a look at just a few examples.

Jesus commands us to love one another in the same way that he has loved us. Why? Because 'by this everyone will know that you are my disciples, if you love one another' (John 13:34–35). This kind of love is a choice to be patient, kind, humble, considerate and selfless, no matter who we are with; it's a conscious determination not to envy, boast, erupt with anger or hold grudges, no matter how we are treated (1 Corinthians 13:4–7). As we live a life of love, the nature of our Lord will be made obvious to others.

We are to live holy lives

The writer to the Hebrews instructs us to live a holy lifestyle. Why? Because 'without holiness no one will see the Lord' (Hebrews 12:14). Walking in step with the ways of the Holy Spirit—in love, joy, peace, patience, kindness, goodness, faithfulness, gentleness and self-control (Galatians 5:22–23) —isn't just a means to please God; it's the path we need to tread so that our lives will be lived to the praise of his glory (Ephesians 1:12, 14). It's how the Word continues to be made flesh today.

Furthermore, we read, 'See to it that no one misses the grace of God and that no bitter root grows up to cause trouble and defile many' (Hebrews 12:15). Do people miss seeing the grace of God as we veil it from view with resentments, unforgiveness or disunity?

We are to be channels for God's power

Jesus said, 'I have given you authority to trample on snakes and scorpions and to overcome all the power of the enemy; nothing will harm you' (Luke 10:19). Supernatural power (for example, casting out demons or healing the sick) can never arise from our own efforts, but God constantly looks for suitable avenues by which he can touch earth with the might of heaven. As we seek to walk in the ways of his Spirit, we provide the channels through which he can display his powerful works.

I pray that, as we reflect on the Word of God and relate to him accordingly, he may be made flesh through our lives in ever-increasing measure. So let us 'be imitators of God… as dearly loved children and live a life of love, just as Christ loved us and gave himself up for us as a fragrant offering and sacrifice to God' (Ephesians 5:1–2).

✳

TAKE IT FURTHER

Reflect

The Word became flesh and made his dwelling among us. We have seen his glory, the glory of the One and Only, who came from the Father, full of grace and truth. (John 1:14)

The glory of the Lord refers to the presence of God. Is the Word being made flesh in me, thereby revealing the presence of God as my life displays his grace and my words express his truth?

Pray

Father God, I regret that too often I've marred the image of Christ in my life, possibly even bringing disrepute to your glorious name. I long to keep in better step with the ways of your Holy Spirit, and I now open my heart to your conviction and forgiveness. May you be made known increasingly through my everyday life.

Read

Genesis 1:1–31; John 1:1–18

woman alive

Celebrating **30** years

Woman Alive is Britain's only independent, monthly woman's magazine specifically for Christian women.

It covers all denominations and seeks to inspire, encourage and resource women in their faith, helping them to grow in their relationship with God and providing practical help and a biblical perspective on the issues impacting their lives.

Find out more at www.womanalive.co.uk or call 01903 604307 for subscription details.

A SPACIOUS PLACE

Contemplating the second half of life

ALIE STIBBE

Alie Stibbe's first book, *Barefoot in the Kitchen*, charted her personal search for God's presence and purpose in the middle of the hectic daily routines of caring for young children. Her long-awaited sequel, *A Spacious Place*, encourages women to prepare for the different challenge of moving to the next stage of life, into a 'spacious place' where new opportunities for personal growth and development can begin to unfold.

The book examines the tension between seeing our destiny as shaped by our own efforts and, by contrast, understanding it as the good things God has in store for us, even as we go through times of emotional, physical and spiritual transition. It also explores how we can move from focusing on the idea of 'success' to valuing what is truly of significance, as we reach a different phase of our working lives.

ISBN 978 1 84101 605 4   £6.99
Available from your local Christian bookshop or direct from BRF: visit www.brfonline.org.uk

Also available as a Kindle edition and ebook.

SHAPING THE HEART

Reflections on spiritual formation and fruitfulness

PAMELA EVANS

God created the human heart to be a worship-filled, holy place with himself in residence, a garden in which the fruit of the Spirit may grow. *Shaping the Heart* is a book for every Christian who wants their heart to become—through the healing and redemptive touch of heavenly grace and mercy—a place where God delights to dwell.

Shaping the Heart is designed for practical use, whether as individual reading for a retreat or quiet day or for shared study and discussion in a group setting. The book considers different aspects of our lives in the light of Christian teaching and looks at how God can touch and transform us through his Spirit, so that we become fruitful disciples. Chapters conclude with three Bible reflections as a springboard to further prayer and reflection.

ISBN 978 1 84101 726 6   £7.99
Available from your local Christian bookshop or direct from BRF: visit www.brfonline.org.uk

RHYTHMS OF GRACE

Finding intimacy with God in a busy life

TONY HORSFALL

Rhythms of Grace emerges from a personal exploration of contemplative spirituality. Coming from an evangelical and charismatic background, Tony Horsfall felt an increasing desire to know God more deeply. At the same time, he felt an increasing dissatisfaction with his own spiritual life, as well as concern at the number of highly qualified and gifted people involved in Christian ministry who experience burn-out.

In this book he shows how contemplative spirituality, with its emphasis on realising our identity as God's beloved children and on being rather than doing, has vital lessons for us about discovering intimacy with God. It also provides essential insights about building a ministry that is both enjoyable and sustainable.

ISBN 978 1 84101 842 3   £7.99
Available from your local Christian bookshop or direct from BRF: visit www.brfonline.org.uk

WORKING FROM A PLACE OF REST

Jesus and the key to sustaining ministry

TONY HORSFALL

Exhaustion, burnout, tiredness, even breakdown… sadly, such conditions are all too common these days, not least among those involved in some kind of Christian ministry. In striving to do our utmost for God, we can easily forget that there were many times when Jesus himself was willing to rest, to do nothing except wait for the Spirit's prompting, so that he demonstrated the vital principle of 'working from a place of rest'.

Drawing on extensive experience of training and mentoring across the world, Tony Horsfall reflects on the story of Jesus and the Samaritan woman to draw out practical guidance for sustainable Christian life and work. As he writes: 'Take some time out to reflect on how you are living and working. Watch Jesus and see how he does it. Listen to what the Spirit may be saying to you deep within; and maybe, just maybe, God will give you some insights that will change your life and sustain your ministry over the long haul.'

ISBN 978 1 84101 544 6   £6.99
Available from your local Christian bookshop or direct from BRF: visit www.brfonline.org.uk

TIME FOR REFLECTION

Meditations to use through the year

ANN PERSSON

It is not easy to switch from activity to stillness, from noise to silence, from achieving to letting go, from doing to being in the presence of God. This book of biblically rooted meditations provides accessible and practical routes to exploring prayer as that way of being in God's presence, letting the sediment of our lives settle so that we may have a true reflection of ourselves and of God within us.

Loosely based around the seasons of the Church year and also drawing inspiration from the seasons of nature, the meditations range from short 'spaces for grace' to longer exercises that can form the basis for a personal quiet day or retreat.

ISBN 978 1 84101 876 8   £8.99
Available from your local Christian bookshop or direct from BRF:
visit www.brfonline.org.uk

MEET JESUS

A call to adventure

JOHN TWISLETON

To engage with Jesus expands the mind and heart. It challenges our view of the way the world is, where it is heading and what difference we could make to it. But in a world of competing philosophies, where does Jesus fit in? How far can we trust the Bible and the Church? What difference does Jesus make to our lives and communities? Is Jesus really the be all and end all?

Meet Jesus is a lively and straightforward exploration of these and other questions, with the aim of engaging our reason, inspiring our faith and worship, deepening our fellowship and service, and bringing new depth to our witness to the world. Each chapter ends with some practical points for action and the book concludes with a section of discussion material for groups.

ISBN 978 1 84101 895 9   £7.99
Available from your local Christian bookshop or direct from BRF:
visit www.brfonline.org.uk

WHOLE LIFE, WHOLE BIBLE

50 readings on living in the light of Scripture

ANTONY BILLINGTON
with MARGARET KILLINGRAY and HELEN PARRY

Where we spend most of our time—at home, at work, in the neighbourhood—matters to God and to his mission in and for the world. Far from restricting our faith to the 'personal' sphere, disengaged from everyday living, Scripture encourages us to take the Lord of life into the whole of life.

Whole Life, Whole Bible is written from the conviction that God's word illuminates every part of existence, enabling us to see differently and live differently—from Monday to Sunday, in public as well as in private. A walk through the unfolding story of the Bible in 50 readings and reflections shows how our lives are bound up with, and shaped by, God's plan to restore a broken universe.

ISBN 978 1 84101 842 3   £7.99
Available from your local Christian bookshop or direct from BRF: visit www.brfonline.org.uk

Also available as a Kindle edition and ebook.

Enjoyed

this book?

Write a review—we'd love to hear what you think.
Email: reviews@brf.org.uk

Keep up to date—receive details of our new books as they happen.
Sign up for email news and select your interest groups at:
www.brfonline.org.uk/findoutmore/

Follow us on Twitter @brfonline

By post—to receive new title information by post (UK only), complete
the form below and post to: BRF Mailing Lists, 15 The Chambers, Vineyard,
Abingdon, Oxfordshire, OX14 3FE

Your Details
Name _____
Address_____
_____
Town/City _____ Post Code _____
Email_____

Your Interest Groups (*Please tick as appropriate)	
☐ Advent/Lent	☐ Messy Church
☐ Bible Reading & Study	☐ Pastoral
☐ Children's Books	☐ Prayer & Spirituality
☐ Discipleship	☐ Resources for Children's Church
☐ Leadership	☐ Resources for Schools

Support your local bookshop
Ask about their new title information schemes.